HAPPINESS WILL FOLLOW YOU

ETERNITY'S BLUE BIRD SERIES

★

Tejvan Pettinger, *Happiness will follow you*

HAPPINESS
WILL
FOLLOW YOU

TEJVAN PETTINGER

WITH CONTRIBUTIONS BY
NIRBHASA MAGEE

SELECTED STORIES BY
SRI CHINMOY

NARZAN CO.
LXXXI

Second edition – August 2011

ISBN 978-88-6606-102-1

TABLE OF CONTENTS

CONTENTS

INTRODUCTION

I wrote these articles over a period of 12 months. Part of the motivation for writing them was that I found the act of writing helpful for my own spiritual life. Of course, writing and reading about what you should be doing is the easy part, but actually living them and putting them into practise is the real test.

Many of the quotes in this book are from my spiritual teacher, Sri Chinmoy. As a student of Sri Chinmoy I have learnt a great deal about meditation and how to live a more peaceful life.

After writing the book, I decided to also include a few stories by Sri Chinmoy on the theme of self-improvement (in Part I and Part VII). These are from his wonderful book, *The Mind-Jungles and The Heart-Gardens of Life* published on August 27th 2001.

*

I hope you get inspiration from this book to help you make some practical changes which make life less stressful and more peaceful. I would like to thank my co-author, Nirbhasa Magee who collaborated in writing articles[1], Vilas Silverton for the beautiful cover art, and Priyadarshan Bontempi who offered encouragement to make the book.

---

[1] The following were written by Nirbhasa: *How to Face up to your Weaknesses and Overcome Them, The Unexpected Power of Gratitude, How to Distinguish Between Love and Emotional Dependence, So, You Think You're Enlightened?, The Many Facets of Forgiveness, An Easy to Learn Concentration Exercise,* and *Learning to Live In The Heart.*

ABOUT THE AUTHORS

Nirbhasa Magee lives in Dublin where he gives meditation classes as a member of the Dublin Sri Chinmoy Centre. Nirbhasa has a PhD in astrophysics, and works as a web consultant and web designer.

Tejvan Pettinger lives in Oxford, where he studied PPE at Lady Margaret Hall, University of Oxford. He works as an economics teacher and writer. He is a member of the Oxford Sri Chinmoy Centre and offers free meditation classes in the city. He is also a member of the Sri Chinmoy Cycling Team and competes in cycle races.

Sri Chinmoy

ABOUT SRI CHINMOY

Born Chinmoy Kumar Ghose in 1931, in the small village of Shakpura in East Bengal (now Bangladesh), Sri Chinmoy was the youngest of seven children. In 1944, after both his parents had passed away, 12 year-old Chinmoy entered the Sri Aurobindo Ashram, a spiritual community near Pondicherry in South India. In his early teens, Chinmoy had many profound inner experiences, and in subsequent years achieved very sublime states of meditation. In 1964, he moved to New York City to share his inner wealth with sincere seekers in the West.

Sri Chinmoy frequently travelled throughout the world to offer free concerts, lectures and public meditations, to meet with his students, and to meet and discuss spirituality with world and community leaders. His spiritual guidance, concerts, lectures and public meditations were always offered free of charge. On the morning of 11 October 2007, Sri Chinmoy entered Mahasamadhi, the mystic process through which spiritual Masters leave the body.

Sri Chinmoy continues to serve as spiritual guide to students in some 60 countries around the world, advocating a balanced lifestyle that incorporates the inner disciplines of prayer and meditation with the dynamism of contemporary life.

PART I

THE MIND-JUNGLES AND
THE HEART-GARDENS OF LIFE

Sri Chinmoy

THE SECRET OF A WORRY-FREE MAN

THERE WAS a man who was worry-free. One day a friend of his asked him, "How is it that you do not have any worries or anxieties?"

The man said, "I know how to deal with worries and anxieties. You people do not know how to deal with worries and anxieties. That is why you suffer."

The friend said to him, "Then please, please teach us. Tell us your secret!"

He said, "All my worries and anxieties I write down on pieces of paper. Then what do I do? I put them in a box and tell myself that on Saturday I will deal with them. On other days I will not deal with worries and anxieties at all.

"Only on Saturdays will I open up the box and pick up a few worries. I see that by then most of my worries have gone away. Only one or two are left. Then I put them back into the box and say to myself, 'These couple of worries I can deal with next week.'

"In the meantime, during the following week, when new worries are coming, again I put them into the box. Then the following Saturday, once again, most of the ones I pick up are no longer worries!

"Always keep a fixed day to deal with worries. You will see that by that day so many worries have disappeared. You will pick them up on that day, and the one or two that remain, you simply put back. When the following week comes, you find that the few old worries have also gone away."

In life, it is always good to have a special time to deal with problems. When that time comes, most of the problems will have already gone away.

Sri Chinmoy

THE TIE AND THE HANDKERCHIEF

ONE DAY a tie and a handkerchief were having an unfortunate dispute. Although the handkerchief did not want to argue, the tie did.

The tie told the handkerchief, "You are useless! You just hide in somebody's pocket, but I show the world how great I am. I make the person very great! I am so dignified, but you are only hiding! The whole world admires me, and you are so insignificant!"

The handkerchief said, "What you are saying makes me so sad. God made me humble. When people shed tears, I wipe them away. People need me and I am so happy to be of service to them. When people are sweating, they take me out of their pockets to wipe their brow. When they cough, they use me. Then again, when they are finished with me, they put me back. I want to be always a humble servitor."

The tie replied, "You are truly useless! Look at how people appreciate and admire me. As soon as someone wears me, I get the whole world's admiration. I cannot imagine how you can ever be happy."

The handkerchief replied, "I am serving in my own humble, modest way. Yes, I am very happy. If you are happy by drawing attention from the world, then please be happy in your way."

"I am telling you once again, you are worse than useless!" proclaimed the tie.

At that very moment God appeared before them. The tie started telling God, "How great I am! Everyone admires me."

The handkerchief said, "Lord, I am so grateful that you have allowed me to be of service by wiping people's tears, and helping them when they are sweating and coughing. You have given me this golden opportunity to serve You, my Lord. I am so grateful."

The tie was very proud! "I am so great! I draw the whole world's attention."

The tie added, "God, tell us! Who is more important? Me or this utterly insignificant handkerchief?"

God said, "My son, my handkerchief is infinitely more important, because he is humble. I created the world for humble service. This is what my handkerchief is doing; whereas, you are not serving humanity. You are only showing off. In my judgement, a handkerchief is infinitely more important than a tie. I want everybody to serve My Creation with utmost humility."

PART II

SELF IMPROVEMENT

A NEGATIVE MINDSET

It is too easy to get into a negative mindset which invariably leads to unhappiness and depression. To avoid being overwhelmed by negativity, we need to make a conscious effort to avoid the experience. When life seems like a perpetual dark tunnel, these are some suggestions to help change your outlook on life.

DON'T CHERISH DESTRUCTIVE THOUGHTS

Often we don't realise how much we subconsciously cherish negative thoughts. It may seem counterintuitive, but a negative frame of mind can occur because we won't let go of the negative thoughts and ideas. The mind clings onto these thoughts with a feeling of self-pity or injured pride. We don't like the negative frame of mind, but at the same time, are we consciously trying to overcome it? The problem is that when the negative thoughts go round and round in our mind, they become powerful and we lose a sense of perspective. We need to make a conscious decision to ignore this flow of negative thoughts and sentiments and be persistent in detaching from negativity.

DO YOU WANT TO BE HAPPY OR MISERABLE?

We should feel that a negative mindset is a choice. If we feel a victim to our own emotions and thoughts, nobody else will be able to help us. By holding onto a negative frame of mind, we are inevitably choosing to be unhappy; each negative thought is a conscious decision to be miserable. If we really value the importance of our own inner peace and happiness, we will aspire to cultivate this through good, uplifting thoughts. Next time you feel the onset of a depressed state of mind, just ask yourself the question: Do I want to be happy or miserable?

SPEND TIME WITH POSITIVE PEOPLE

The best antidote to negativity is simply to spend time doing positive, uplifting activities. Sometimes, if we analyse and examine our own negativity it does nothing to reduce it. By engaging in useful, fun activities we forget about the reasons for our negativity; this is often a powerful way to overcome a depressed state of mind.

DON'T ACCEPT NEGATIVITY FROM OTHER PEOPLE

We live in a world where there are no shortages of pessimists, critics and doom-mongers. There will always be people who can find the negative in life, but we do not have to subscribe to their world view. For example, when people have a negative attitude to their workplace, even if there are faults and limitations, we need not allow them to make us a negative person.

LET GO OF THOUGHTS

If you can learn to control your thoughts, you can control the experience and emotions of life. The best antidote to negativity is learning the art of meditation. Meditation is more than just relaxation; it is a change in consciousness, whereby we move from the limited perspective of our mind and discover an inner source of happiness.

LIVE IN THE HEART

The nature of the mind is to be suspicious and critical. If someone does 99 good things and one bad thing, the mind will invariably remember the bad thing. If we allow ourselves to be drawn into highlighting the mistakes of others we will invite a negative mindset. However, if we live in the heart we are not drawn to the faults of others.

It is in the heart that we can have a true sense of oneness with others; when we are in the heart the faults of others seem insignificant, and we can feel a sense of identity with their achievements.

DON'T SIT AROUND DOING NOTHING

The worst thing for a negative frame of mind is to mope around feeling sorry for ourselves. Ruminating on our bad luck / worries / fears will not diminish them in any way. Physical exercise can be a powerful way to bring about a change in our low consciousness. Negativity is often associated with boredom and lack of purpose. Rather than endlessly checking emails and surfing the web, it is better look for something good to do.

THINK OF THREE POSITIVE THOUGHTS

If you are feeling really miserable and have a low sense of self-esteem, try thinking of three good things that you have done. At times our own mind can be our worst enemy and very self-critical. It is important not to lose a sense of balance; for the various bad things we have done, we have also done some good things.

DON'T THINK ANYTHING
YOU WOULDN'T SAY IN FRONT OF PEOPLE

We often think things we would never say in front of people. If you are annoyed or disappointed with someone, imagine what you would say to him or her in person. Sometimes when we are with people we are forced to behave; even if we are not particularly sincere, the effort to avoid negativity can help us to overcome our bad mood.

INNER PEACE

Inner peace is the most valuable thing that we can cultivate. Nobody can give us inner peace; at the same time, it is only our own thoughts that can rob us of it. To experience inner peace, we don't have to retreat to a Himalayan cave; we can experience inner peace right now, exactly where we are. The most important criteria is to value the importance of inner peace. If we really value inner peace, we will work hard to make it a reality.

These are some suggestions for bringing more peace into your mind.

CHOOSE CAREFULLY WHERE WE SPEND TIME

If you are a news addict and spend an hour reading newspapers everyday, your mind will be agitated by the relentless negativity you see in the world. It is possible to detach from this negativity but in practice, we make our progress easier if we don't spend several hours ruminating over the problems of the world. If you have a spare 15 minutes, don't automatically switch on the TV or surf the internet. Take the opportunity to be still or at least do something positive. The problem is that the mind feels insecure unless it has something to occupy it. When we can attain a clear mind, however, we discover that it creates a genuine sense of happiness and inner peace.

CONTROL OF THOUGHTS

It is our thoughts that determine our state of mind. If we constantly cherish negative and destructive thoughts, inner peace will always remain a far cry. At all costs, we need to avoid pursuing trains of negative thoughts. This requires practise, as we cannot attain mastery of our thoughts overnight. At the same time, we always have to remember that we can decide which thoughts to follow and which to reject. Never feel you are a helpless victim to your thoughts.

> If you have inner peace, nobody can force you to be a slave to the outer reality .[2]

SIMPLIFY YOUR LIFE

Modern life places great demands on our time. We may feel that we never have enough time to accomplish all our tasks. However, we should seek to minimise these outer demands and to take time to simplify our life. There are many things that we can do without; quite often we add unnecessary responsibilities to our schedule. Do the most significant tasks one at a time and enjoy doing them. To experience inner peace, it is essential to avoid cluttering our life with unnecessary activities and worries.

SPEND TIME TO CULTIVATE INNER PEACE

As we might spend 8 hours a day to earn money, can we not spend 15 minutes a day to cultivate inner peace? No matter how much money we earn, it cannot bring us inner peace; but if we spent 15 minutes practising meditation and relaxation, inner peace can become a possibility. Meditation does not just mean sitting still for

---

[2] Sri Chinmoy, Peace, New York: Agni Press, 1985

30 minutes; we actually seek to experience a state of consciousness which is flooded with inner peace. To experience this inner peace, we cannot allow any thought to enter into our mind. True inner peace takes place when we can transcend the world of thoughts.

> *You cannot buy peace;*
> *You must know how to manufacture it within, in the still-*
> *ness of your daily practises in meditation .*[3]

BE IMMUNE TO FLATTERY AND CRITICISM

If we depend on the opinions and praise of other people, we can never have inner peace. Criticism and flattery are two sides of the same coin, both the judgements of others and we should not allow ourselves to be affected by either. When we are very sensitive to the opinions of others, we feed the ego. Better that we learn to have confidence in ourselves, which does not mean loving ourselves in an egotistical way. It requires us to value our real self and have belief in the good qualities that are part of everyone.

BE ACTIVE SELFLESSLY

Inner peace does not mean that we have to live the life of a hermit. Inner peace can be felt amidst dynamic activity, but this action should be performed with selfless motives. When we serve others, we forget our sense of self, and it is when we forget our limited self that we can have inner peace.

---

[3] Paramahansa Yogananda, Inner Peace — How to be Calmly Active and Actively Calm, Los Angeles: Self-Realization Fellowship, 1999

AVOID CRITICISING OTHERS

We should feel that to have our inner peace depends on the well being of others. If we are indifferent to the feelings of others, then it is impossible to have inner peace for ourselves. What we give out, comes back: if we offer a peaceful attitude to others then this is what we will see return.

HOW TO OVERCOME YOUR WEAKNESSES

Often we have a rather fixed concept of ourselves, and how we would like others to perceive us. Hence, it's a pretty painful experience when you are suddenly confronted with some unsavoury aspect of your nature, and it's doubly painful when it's exposed for all to see. Some of us become resigned to saying "that's just the way I am" and claiming their weakness almost as a badge of identity, whereas others go to the opposite extreme, mentally flagellating themselves for every misstep they make in life.

Is there a middle path between these two extremes? Can you really overcome your weaknesses? From the changes I have seen in my life, and also from watching the lives of many of my friends who in one form or another have committed themselves to truly living at their fullest potential, I can definitely say yes to these two questions. And like many other things, it's a question of how you do it. Here are a few observations:

DWELLING ON YOUR WEAKNESS ONLY GIVES IT STRENGTH

When we hate other people, what happens? The thought of them pervades our mental space, and ends up unconsciously guiding our emotions and actions. Similarly, forever thinking of how bad your weaknesses are gives them power over you, and make you feel helpless in the face of them. It is better to always keep an attitude of pragmatism - the bad thing you did in the past cannot be changed now, but you can always work on avoiding a repeat in the future.

SELF-ACCEPTANCE

We often set unrealistic ideas of the person we should be, and newly discovered weaknesses often cause us pain because it jarringly conflicts with this idea. The first step in overcoming weaknesses is to lose these unrealistic ideas and accept yourself as you actually are. By accepting yourself, warts and all, you are not giving up. No, it is in fact a realistic assessment of where you stand now in your life. Once you have learned to accept and love yourself as you are, you can then work on the journey of self-improvement.

YOU ARE NOT YOUR PROBLEMS

When we are confronted with a particular weakness, it tends to crowd our mind making us feel that we are the sum total of our weaknesses! This is absolutely not true. If a cloud temporarily covers the sun, it does not mean that the sun does not exist. Your problems are not "you"; they are merely temporary limitations and bad habits obstructing your true nature, and as such, can always be unlearned and transformed.

FOCUS ON INCREASING THE POSITIVE QUALITY

It is always a much more rewarding task to increase positive qualities than reduce negative ones. If, for instance, you lose your temper easily, you can focus on increasing your inner calmness. If you are prone to criticising others, try and increase the number of good things you see in everyone you meet. Working on positive goals turns the situation around from a struggle with "the enemy within" to a process of inner growth and blossoming.

NEVER GIVE UP

The process of human improvement is not like making instant coffee or a taking miracle pill. There are ups and downs and times when it may be difficult to see clear progress. Yet, bear in mind that anything we did that ever brought us a feeling of joy and satisfaction, only came because we committed to it and saw it through to the end.

HOW TO OVERCOME ANGER

Here are some practical suggestions for dealing with anger.

WHEN YOU ARE ANGRY SAY NOTHING

If we speak in anger we will definitely aggravate the situation and quite likely hurt the feelings of others. If we speak in anger we will find that people respond in the same manner, creating a spiral of the negative force, anger. If we can remain outwardly silent, it allows time for the emotion of anger to leave us.

> *When angry, count to ten before you speak. If very angry, count to one hundred. .*[4]

BE INDIFFERENT TO THOSE WHO SEEK TO MAKE US ANGRY

Some people may unfortunately take a malicious pleasure in trying to make us mad. However, if we can feel indifferent to them and their words, if we feel it is beyond our dignity to even acknowledge them, then their words and actions will have no effect. Also, if we do not respond in any way to their provocation, they will lose interest and not bother us in the future.

---

[4] Thomas Jefferson, Letter to the infant Thomas Jefferson Smith, 21 February 1825

USE REASON TO STOP ANGER

When you feel anger coming to the fore, try to take a step back and say to yourself "This anger will not help me in any way. This anger will make the situation worse." Even if part of us remains angry, our inner voice is helping us to distance ourself from the emotion of anger.

LOOK KINDLY UPON OTHERS

A visualisation you could try is to see the anger-rousing agent as a five-year-old child. If you think of the other person as a helpless five-year-old child, your compassion and forgiveness will come to the fore. If your baby brother accidentally injured you, there would be no feeling of anger and a desire to retaliate. Instead, you would just feel he is just too young to know any better. This exercise may be particularly useful for close members of the family who at times evoke your anger.

VALUE PEACE MORE THAN ANGER

If we value peace of mind as our most important treasure we will not allow anger to remain in our system. As Sri Chinmoy says:

> You may have every right to be angry with someone, but you know that by getting angry with him you will only lose your precious peace of mind. .[5]

---

[5] Sri Chinmoy, The Illumination Of Life-Clouds, Part 2, New York: Agni Press, 1974

DETACHMENT

When you feel the need to defend yourself from others' criticisms, if you can remain detached and calm they may begin to feel guilty about venting their anger on you. Inspired by your example of calmness, they will seek subconsciously to do the same.

FOCUS ON SOMETHING COMPLETELY DIFFERENT

Suppose someone has done something to make you angry. Think about something that will make you happy. The best antidote to negativity is to focus on the positive.

BREATHE DEEPLY

The simple act of breathing deeply will help considerably with removing anger.

MEDITATION

Practise meditation regularly to bring forward your inner peace. If we know how to access our inner peace, we will be able to draw upon this during testing times.

SMILE

To smile is offer goodwill to others. Smiling costs nothing, yet by smiling we can effectively defuse many tense, negative situations.

TIPS TO AVOID BECOMING DEPRESSED

Is it possible to avoid depression? What is the secret of cultivating happiness and avoiding periods of unhappiness? To a large extent, we determine our own frame of mind and we should not feel that we are a helpless victim to depression. Depression is something that we can avoid by cultivating the opposite - happiness.

Here are some tips for avoiding depression.

OFFER GOODWILL TO OTHERS

If we seek to make others miserable how can we expect to be happy ourselves? Offering goodwill to other people creates a powerful positive energy. Focusing on other people's good qualities can definitely help improve our own state of mind. There is a universal principle that what we give out, we get back.

Therefore, by offering positive energy to others, at some time, we will also be the recipients.

LEARN TO DETACH FROM THOUGHTS

Thoughts play a very significant role in determining our state of mind. If we pursue negative thoughts then we give them greater power and influence over our state of being. However, it is possible to decide which thoughts to allow and which to reject. We have to learn to be vigilant and prevent negative thoughts from taking hold in our mind. As soon as we become aware of negative thoughts we should let go of them. We can imagine that we are throwing them out of our mind into a cosmic dustbin.

KEEP BUSY

If we struggle to detach from negative thoughts we should just throw ourselves into other activities. Getting involved in other activities that we enjoy takes us out of ourselves. Activity enables us to do something constructive, and allows us not to dwell on our depressed state of mind.

AVOID FEELINGS OF GUILT

Harbouring feelings of guilt after making a mistake will not help alleviate the situation. In particular, we should avoid feeling guilty for minor events of no significance. Instead of feeling guilty, we should seek to concentrate on doing the right thing.

LIVE A BALANCED LIFE

We need to make room for different aspects in our life. Focussing all our time and energy on work leaves no time for relaxation and enriching activities. Unhappiness is more likely to result if we pursue an unbalanced life.

DON'T BASE YOUR HAPPINESS SOLELY ON OTHER PEOPLE

If we expect to gain happiness from another person, at some time, we are bound to be disappointed. If bad relationships end, we should see it as an opportunity to move on.

It is not helpful to dwell on what might have been. It is also a mistake to feel that we can change somebody to match our preferences. By seeking to change a person fundamentally, we will only feel frustrated when we fail.

SHARE PROBLEMS

Whilst good friendships can offer tremendous help, our friends will not always be able to solve our problems. However, simply having someone to talk to and share difficulties greatly helps in being able to work through our own problems.

CULTIVATE HAPPINESS

To avoid depression, we need to focus on the alternative which is happiness. The problem is that when we are depressed, the idea of happiness seems a million miles away. At such times, if we can force a smile or try to be insincerely happy, we can trick the mind and compel happiness to emerge and after a while we start to feel real happiness.

Happiness
Will follow you
If your heart remains
Undisturbed by trifles.[6]

HAVE LOW EXPECTATIONS

Depression often occurs because our desires remain unfulfilled. The more desires we have, the more likely we are to be disappointed. After disappointment comes a sense of frustration and depression. Minimising our desires will not make us prone to disappointment, nor does it prevent us from striving for excellence and achieving various goals. However, it helps to have an attitude of detachment to the outcome.

DON'T DWELL ON THE NEGATIVE

This is the key to avoiding depression. If we focus always on negative things this will eventually filter through into our state of mind. Negativity can come from miserable people, depressing situations and our own negative thoughts. If we want to cultivate happiness, we should seek to avoid depressing situations and depressing people.

---

[6] Sri Chinmoy, Ten Thousand Flower-Flames, Part 77, #7666. New York: Agni Press, 1983

HOW TO AVOID
BECOMING A GRUMPY OLD MAN

In the UK, there is a TV series "Grumpy Old Men," supposedly a comedy programme, where middle-aged men complain about everything from the price of petrol to the overbearing popularity of American Idol. In a way their complaints are mildly amusing, but it did get me thinking — Is that how I want to be in 20–30 years time — always complaining and being grumpy? Often we see people who, in their early life, have a sympathetic, hopeful and positive attitude of mind. Thirty years later, however, those positive qualities have slowly been eroded and replaced with a propensity towards being grumpy, miserable and negative. How can we ensure that we avoid the "grumpy old man" syndrome and remain positive throughout our advancing years?

DON'T GET STUCK IN A RUT

When we get stuck in a rut, life seems listless and boring. With a lack of newness in our own life, we have more time to observe the failings of others, the world and ourselves. If you find yourself always complaining about the same things in life, try to do something different. Unfortunately, it is possible to develop a subtle enjoyment of being negative. The mind gets a certain misplaced pleasure by being grumpy and complaining, but this kind of happiness is extremely limited. Look for ways to observe life in a new way; remain dynamic and don't leave yourself time to become overwhelmed with negativity. If necessary, force yourself to try a completely new skill or activity.

DON'T GET EXASPERATED OVER THINGS YOU CANNOT CONTROL

If the price of oil increases, there is not much you can do about it. Just because you incessantly complain about the price of oil, Saudi Arabia is not going to start producing an extra 10 million barrels a day. If you get upset at things like this, you will invariably make yourself miserable. To some extent, we have to be accepting of external situations beyond our control. For example, Governments always have done and always will do things which are unpopular; we can't expect this to change. What we can do is change our attitude. Rather than getting worked up by these things, we can develop a greater sense of detachment. Don't allow your life to be dominated by complaints about the outside world.

HAVE THE PERSPECTIVE OF A YOUNG CHILD

We never refer to "grumpy young children". True, a child may have a temporary bad mood, but they will soon shake it off. To a child the world is simple and a place of wonder. Life is not complicated but something to enjoy. A child does not spend his time criticising things; he just plays and enjoys life. We may feel that as sophisticated adults we must be much better, but can moving from a childlike positive attitude to a miserable attitude be seen as progress? It doesn't matter how old we are; what matters is our inner attitude. If we can feel we have a childlike heart, it helps considerably in avoiding grumpiness. Even observing the simple smile of a child helps put a smile on our face.

LEAVE CRITICISM TO OTHERS

Criticism and grumpiness are intricately linked. If we spend all our time criticising and gossiping about others, we will develop a negative mindset. It is easy to find things to criticise in this world and even after spending all day judging and criticising other people, we would not have got very far. The world does not change as a result of our astute criticisms of others. What happens is that as we criticise the world, it gives us a subconscious feeling of superiority and this motivates us to spend even more time criticising. If we want real happiness, we have to take a positive attitude and look for good things to encourage — in other words, make a positive contribution. The world does not need more grumpy old men; there will always be plenty of people ready to complain about the level of taxes. What the world needs is people who will help make a positive difference.

BE FLEXIBLE

As we get older, if we are not careful, we become more inflexible: we want and expect things to be done in a certain way and it be-comes more difficult for us to accept change. This rigid attitude can make us very grumpy when things don't go as we expect. On the other hand, imagine a tree, whose branches are flexible and sway in the wind. If they couldn't bend they would snap. It is im-portant that as we age, we do not become "stuck in our ways" but remain flexible.

SELF AWARENESS

Grumpiness and a negative attitude often creep up on us without our realising it and only after some time do we become aware of feeling depressed and unhappy. We don't immediately realise it is because of our own negative mental attitude, clearly something important to be aware of. If we really want to remain cheerful and positive, then we can make it happen by evaluating our attitude towards life — if you are becoming a grumpy old man, make a resolution to change.

POSITIVE ATTITUDE

If we want to avoid being miserable, the most effective strategy is to focus on the opposite, the positive side of life. Instead of criticising people, try to look for good qualities to encourage. Instead of thinking of the things you can't do, try beginning new activities and initiatives. A positive attitude will also be easier if we remain busy and dynamic. It is easier for the critical mind to predominate when we are idle.

GETTING OUT OF A RUT

If you find yourself stuck in a rut, life can become monotonous, dreary and uninspiring. It is easy to feel life is going nowhere, especially if we have problems at work or with family. To bring newness into our lives, we need to first acknowledge that we are actually stuck in a rut. After that we can make a conscious decision to rejuvenate our lives.

Here are some practical tips to get out of a rut.

SET CHALLENGES

The setting and pursuit of personal challenges are a very powerful way of motivating yourself to do something new. If there is no target it is easy to make a half-hearted effort and give up. However, when we have something very clear to aim for, it is much more likely we will actually make something happen.

FOCUS ON THE PRESENT MOMENT

Do you spend a lot of time regretting the past? Everyone makes decisions they later regret, but if you become consumed with regret you will not be able to move forward from the experience. Don't be preoccupied with the past and future, try to enjoy the present moment.

DO WITHOUT SOME EVERYDAY THINGS

It is easy to get into a routine where we spend several hours doing the same uninspiring activities. If you are addicted to watching TV, surfing the net or playing computer games, make a decision to do without them for a day or week; this will force you to do something completely different. This does not mean you have to give up watching TV completely, but becoming totally absorbed in it leaves no opportunity for discovering newness in life.

LEARN A NEW SKILL

Learning a new skill gives us the opportunity to find a new avenue for creativity and inspiration. In the process of learning we can get a feeling of self-improvement. This is a great antidote to being stuck in a rut.

DO SOMETHING FOR OTHER PEOPLE

When we do something selflessly for other people, we can bring out the best in ourselves. Offering useful service to other people is highly rewarding.

LOOK AT THINGS FROM A DIFFERENT PERSPECTIVE

Experiencing a dull, boring life is often a reflection of our inner attitude. If we have a tendency to be negative, then it is more likely that life feels dreary and flat. For example, try to look at relationships from a different perspective; stop complaining constantly about other people's behaviour; if you wait for other people to behave as you want them to, you will always be frustrated. Instead, practise tolerance and patience.

DON'T LISTEN ENDLESSLY TO YOUR THOUGHTS

It is your own thoughts that make you feel you are stuck in a rut, and that life is boring and futile. But why do you have to listen to these thoughts? Learn to manage your thoughts and let go of these negative opinions. If you can clear your mind, this will make a big difference to your outlook on life.

SPEND TIME WITH ENTHUSIASTIC PEOPLE

When you feel stuck in a rut, try to spend some time with enthusiastic, positive people, as some of their energy will rub off on you. Even if you don't particularly feel like doing it, meeting other people will take you out of yourself and help to re-energise yourself.

DON'T KEEP COMPLAINING

You could spend 24 hours a day complaining about various things, but would that give you any satisfaction? When we complain we actually give both our energy and focus to the negative. Complaining simply makes life seem more dreary and unfair.

HUMOUR

Even in the most banal experiences there is the opportunity for humour. Don't take life too seriously; try to see the funny side. Without humour the world would probably have ended long ago.

HOW TO REDUCE THE EGO

The ego is that part in us which feeds off praise, compliments and success. When we live in the ego we are inevitably subject to feelings of superiority and inferiority, pride and worthlessness, success and failure. If we want to avoid these negative emotions we need to transcend the ego. If we can transcend the ego, we will find that people are instinctively more attracted to us, even though we are no longer trying to impress. It may seem a great paradox, yet limiting the role of our ego can make a radical difference to our lives.

These are some factors which can reduce the power of the Ego.

DON'T TRY TO IMPRESS

Don't boast about your own achievements and avoid forcing your accomplishments and success into the conversation. If you have been successful in accumulating wealth, try to keep quiet about it. All these factors may impress your own ego, but you can guarantee they will have little positive impact on other people.

BE AWARE OF FALSE MODESTY

Sometimes when we say, "Oh, I'm absolutely hopeless" actually what we are wanting is for people to respond with "Oh no you're not, you're really good." Humility means that we don't take excessive pride in our achievements, but, it also means we don't exaggerate our failings in the hope of gaining sympathy.

BE CAREFUL OF FLATTERY

We need to be careful about receiving praise, in some ways it can be as difficult as receiving criticism. The ego likes receiving praise and we can easily become addicted to being flattered. Don't seek out people who are keen to flatter us, as this only feeds the ego. Also, be wary of flattering other people in the hope that they will return the compliment.

DON'T USE YOUR RELIGION / SPIRITUALITY TO IMPRESS

It is a mistake to feel that the practise of a religion / spiritual path gives us a moral superiority over other people. If we feel any superiority we are missing the whole point of spirituality. Spirituality is about a feeling of oneness — not of proving that one path is better than others. This can be one of the most insidious types of ego, because when we wrap up the ego in a sense of moral superiority, we can easily trick ourselves into thinking we are reducing the ego, when actually we are strengthening it.

BE AWARE OF THE EXTENDED EGO

Ego is not just about feeling we are better than others as individuals. Our Ego can also be expressed via a national / religious bias, where the same problem of ego exists, but is expressed through an extended sense of identity. It is just as damaging, although we may feel that somehow there is no ego involved because it is not directly related to ourselves.

DON'T SPEAK BADLY OF OTHERS

Quite often, when we speak ill of others there is a subtle attempt to make ourselves look better. We may not explicitly say it, but, when we point to someone's shortcomings we imply that we don't have these, and therefore we are much better than them. The important thing here is the motive. Be very vigilant; what is your inner motive for criticising someone else? It it to make you feel or look better? The irony of course is that when we criticise someone, often we have the same imperfections ourselves — it is just that we find it easier to see them in other people.

WHAT IS YOUR MOTIVATION FOR DOING SOMETHING?

If nobody knew that you had performed a good deed, would you still do it with the same intensity? Can you work without expecting reward and praise? If you can do things selflessly with no desire for people to find out, this is a sign you do not give importance to the ego. If you only do things in the hope of praise, then you are working to satisfy the ego. If you really work selflessly, at some point, your efforts will receive much greater recognition because people will come to also value the selfless motivation behind the action. Try doing some things without letting anyone know about it. In the New Testament, this is what Jesus meant when he said,

"But when you give alms, do not let your left hand know what your right hand is doing" (Matthew 6:1–4).

DON'T RELY ON YOUR PHYSICAL APPEARANCE TO IMPRESS

If you rely on your physical beauty to impress, this is definitely coming from the ego. This is not to see beauty as a bad thing, far from it, but real beauty is heightened by modesty and the absence of ego. Avoid paying excessive interest to your physical looks.

To reduce our ego, we have to give great importance to our thoughts and motivation behind our actions. We have to be strict with ourselves and work out why we are doing something. To reduce the ego, requires great vigilance and the need to reflect on each action and motivation. A reduced influence of the ego is of great value and the key to achieving a sense of inner peace.

THE POWER OF GRATITUDE

In today's fast moving world, qualities such as gratitude seem to belong to another age — a simpler time when life moved along at an easier pace and there was time to appreciate everything. Yet within this apparently meek-sounding quality there lies a tremendous source of power that can radically reshape the way you look at the world.

WHAT GRATITUDE CAN DO FOR US

It puts things in perspective: as human beings have this self-defeating propensity to let the bad things in life fill our mental vision and leave no room for the good, a tendency reflected and perpetuated by television and newspapers. Often it takes just one bad thing to happen for us dwell on it and get depressed, no matter how many good things that are happening. In cultivating a daily practice of gratitude, we start to reverse that process and gain a true perspective on life.

It lifts us above the ebbs and tides of life: The more you develop the quality of gratitude in your life, the more you will start feeling grateful even when bad things happen to you, because you will have developed the inner vision to see that good things and bad happenings are nothing but experiences to shape you and make you stronger. Hence you will be able to have peace of mind no matter what the outer circumstances are.

It takes us out of our limited ego: As with other practices of self-discovery, your awareness expands and you gradually feel you are part of something more vast than your limiting ego and finite mortal frame.

Gratitude helps us turn away from self-centredness and realise our place in the universe. It awakens a higher part of our being: gratitude is primarily a quality felt by the heart centre, situated in the middle of our chest where we can feel our soul, or the essence of our existence. Therefore, when we are consciously grateful, some inmost part of ourselves is awakened and we enter into the higher and nobler realms of our being.

TECHNIQUES TO CULTIVATE THE QUALITY OF GRATITUDE

There are many different techniques to use; the important thing is that they be practised every day, preferably at the same time each day so you can form a habit. Just after you get up in the morning is usually the best time — you are not likely to be disturbed, and the peace and serenity you get from the practice benefits you throughout your whole day.

Writing down things you are grateful for: This serves as a useful beginning to the other techniques. Each day you can write down seven things that you are truly grateful for, and as you write try to feel that quality inside your heart. When you start writing, you realise how many things there are — from the big things such as the gift of life and friends, down to tiny little incidents that happened yesterday such as someone giving you a smile or the chance to spend a few minutes sitting in a park.

Expanding the flower of gratitude inside your heart: you can try silently chanting the word gratitude over and over again. Each time you repeat the word you can feel that a tiny flower of gratitude inside your heart is growing and growing, expanding petal by petal.

Cultivating inner joy: joy carries with it the quality of expansion and awareness which gives rise to gratitude. Try breathing in and out and keeping your awareness on the river of breath entering and leaving your body. Feel that when you breathe in, pure inner joy in entering into your heart, and when you breathe out, worry tension and stress are leaving your system.

REMAINING YOUNG AT HEART

Everyday we look in the mirror and gain the habit of identifying our sense of self with the body. Thus, when we see grey hairs and wrinkles appearing we feel older — because our body is becoming older. Whilst nobody really likes getting older, we can easily remain young at heart — here, our physical appearance is an irrelevance, whatever our age . We need to break the link between our physical condition and state of mind. We try to keep the body healthy, but our sense of self should not be dictated by the number of summers this body has seen. Sometimes we see someone in his twenties and already he is grumbling like an old man. But, at the same time we see someone in there seventies and they have the life and attitude of a young child. To remain young at heart in our old age is a real blessing, which enables us to enjoy life.

SPEND TIME WITH CHILDREN

Children enjoy life from the heart. To see a child's smile uplifts even the most indifferent mood. If we always spend time with serious old people we will feel a serious old person too.

BE SPONTANEOUS

A childlike attitude is spontaneous and free. A child can take joy in simple things because it is not mentally creating a five-year plan to buy a new TV. Try to listen to your heart and do things which give you innocent pleasure. Spend less time thinking and more time living in the present moment.

DON'T SPEND TIME PICKING FAULTS

> *When we criticise others,*
> *We do not go forward.*
> *We just go backward,*
> *To our greatest shock.*[7]

It is complaining and grumbling which really gives us a feeling of being old and weary. Unfortunately, as we get older we get into a mental habit of finding faults and criticising the innumerable problems of the world. It is this tendency to be critical which really gives us an ageing outlook. A critical attitude has an impact upon ourselves. It is we who become negative, yet our criticisms fail to improve the world.

---

[7] Sri Chinmoy, Seventy-Seven Thousand Service-Trees, Part 13, #12753. New York: Agni Press, 1999

BE ACTIVE

If we are active we don't have time to get depressed about our old age. Competing with ourselves and not others enables us to get joy from transcending our own goals.

STOP BEING GUILTY OF YOUR AGE

I know many people close to me, who really feel bad if you ask them how old they are. They tell their age with such reluctance — as if they had just been diagnosed with some serious illness. Be proud to have more experience and more years under your belt. Becoming older in age is nothing to feel bad about.

HOW TO AVOID NEGATIVITY

One of the great challenges in life is to avoid. It is easy to become suspicious, critical, depressed, fearful, but despite the prevailing attitudes of the world there is no inevitability that we have to become a grumpy old man. It is quite possible to see the beautiful in the ordinary and bring to the fore the better side of human nature. If we avoid negativity we will see definitely see the positive in life and enjoy life much more.

CRITICISE NOT

Criticising others is a very pervasive bad habit we all have. Sometimes we can actually go out of our way to look for the failings and faults of others. It is as if we are blind to their good qualities but their mistakes stand out in our mind. Even worse we can often imagine faults that others might have. This is the height of stupidity, but the nature of the mind can easily turn to negativity and we have to be on guard. Rather than being critical, we should try to look for the good qualities in others.

59

To deliberately criticise
Another individual
May cause an indelible stain
On the critic.[8]

The world will not collapse if we halt our self-styled criticism. If we look to encourage and praise the good aspects of others, we will bring these qualities to the fore in ourselves.

CHOOSING CONSCIOUSLY

All the time we are faced with choices. Ask yourself, 'Do I see the negative or the positive?' Somebody at work might pass a thoughtless and disparaging comment. Our instinctive reaction may be to nurse a sense of grievance and think of many equally unpleasant things to say about the person in return. However, another way to look at this situation would be to think, 'They are unfortunately wrong; perhaps they are feeling insecure and so try to unfairly put others down. In the past there may have been times when I may have done something like that. I will make an effort to be kind to that person, as this will be the best way to show they were mistaken and also to help them overcome their depressed state of mind.'

The first response invites a tit-for-tat response which will encourage negativity. The second response is dignified and requires nobility of character. We lose nothing,however, by avoiding negativity — in fact we gain a tremendous amount. The point is that we always have a choice about how we respond to situations; avoiding the negative and unpleasant just takes a conscious decision.

---

[8]   Sri Chinmoy, Twenty-Seven Thousand Aspiration-Plants, #14805. Part 149, 1991

SELF-BELIEF

It is vital to cultivate a sense of self-worth and self-respect. If we do not have faith in ourselves, how can we have faith in anyone else? Self-belief should not be equated with arrogance or pride. We are seeking to cultivate a sense of self-respect so we are at peace with ourselves. We are often our worst critic, sometimes gnoring genuine faults but worrying excessively over minor issues that are not really faults. We need to learn from our mistakes and be honest about our weaknesses, but it should not be at a cost of putting ourselves down. If we make a mistake, learn to let go, don't keep the negative memory at the forefront of your mind. If we can have a good feeling about ourselves, it will be very easy to have a good feeling about others and the rest of the world.

SERVICE

Idleness is the worst cultivator of negativity. If we sit moping aimlessly around we will inevitably become bored and negative. Life will seem to be no fun. The easiest way to change our mindset is to become meaningfully busy. If we really want to serve others there will always be some way that we can find. If we are really busy, we will not have time to criticise the world. If we don't have work to do, we can just take physical exercise, which is an excellent way of shaking off the cobwebs of our mind.

OSMOSIS

The nature of the human mind is that it consciously or unconsciously absorbs the vibrations from around itself. If we spend time with negative people, watching 24-hour news, then we will be more prone to negativity ourselves. We have to choose our work and leisure time carefully. Don't spend too much time with the "grumpy old men" or "gossipy old ladies." When we do spend time with negative people, we need to be on our guard that we don't end up sharing their worldview.

BE YOUNG AT HEART

I have already made two references to "grumpy old men" - this is not an ageist remark. You can be a "grumpy old man" when you are 20 or you can remain young at heart at 80 years old . Age is very much something of a mental attitude. We need to cultivate a childlike attitude which takes joy from small, simple, beautiful things. We need to avoid a great sophistication and mental dissection of everything. By over-analysing life, we would be living in the mind and be unable to live in the heart.

PART III

RELATIONSHIPS

LOVE AND EMOTIONAL DEPENDENCE

The word "love" is perhaps one of the most casually used terms in the English language — so much so that it has become an umbrella term for a whole variety of very different emotions! There is one thing we all agree on — that love is what makes the world go round and, without it, the world is but a dry empty shell of a place. On the other hand, it is a word we very easily twist around to our own purposes to justify our emotional dependence on a person. If we can learn to distinguish love from emotional dependence and put this distinction into practice, then we make life more beautiful not only for us, but for everyone we come into contact with.

LEARN TO LOVE YOURSELF FIRST

Our remedies oft in ourselves do lie, which we ascribe to heaven.[9]

Often when we are emotionally dependent on someone, we are looking to them as a "filler" to cover over and distract us from unresolved emotional issues in ourselves. In order to truly love someone, we first have to discover and explore what love is, and

---

[9] Shakespeare William, All's Well That Ends Well Act I, scene I, Oxford: Oxford Paperbacks, 2008

that means starting with the person you spend the most time with — yourself! We can often name our shortcomings far quicker than our positive qualities, and we are very quick to beat ourselves up for anything we didn't do to our satisfaction. This all has to change. Try every day to identify your positive qualities and increase them, and when you do make a mistake, try and see it as a "work-in-progress" rather than an absolute failure. When your own self-love and self-respect increases, you are then able to approach relationships with others with much more equanimity.

USE THE HEART

Along with the word "love", the word "heart" is often dragged into many conversations and used to describe all manner of behaviour, good and bad. When we talk about the heart we mean the space in the middle of the chest we point to when we say, "this is me" — the place where we feel the essence of our being more than anywhere else. It is also where most of our higher and nobler qualities emanate from — empathy, kindness and love.

Emotional attachment, on the other hand is a tangled up array of feelings from the mind and also from the emotional part of our being, located closer to the navel. Because the sources of love and emotional attachment are located so lose together, they can and are often confused by the undiscerning person. However, setting aside some time each day for a practice of self-discovery and self-enquiry (e.g. meditation) will very quickly enable you to distinguish one from the other.

DON'T EXPECT

> *When your love is pure or spiritual, there is no demand, no expectation. There is only the sweetest feeling of spontaneous oneness with the human being or beings concerned.* [10]

Social anthropologists often describe many human relationships like a contract — we give our love to a person and at the same time we subconsciously place all kinds of expectations on that person which we want them to fulfil. And then when the other person fails to sufficiently satisfy our demands (which will definitely happen from time to time — we're all imperfect), we feel let down and angry with the person, revealing our insecurity and fear of not being loved, and we often resort to some kind of emotional manipulation to try and get them to fulfil our demands.

True love, on the other hand, is like the sun. The sun shines its rays and gives its warmth to all and sundry, without expecting anything in return. This may sound like naivety to the calculating mind, but when we live in the heart we feel exactly like the sun does — we just want spread our love and goodwill anywhere we can. With this kind of love we have detachment — we have no fixed ideas about what way this love should be taken by others; the mere act of giving love satisfies our heart immensely.

---

[10] Sri Chinmoy, Earth's Cry Meets Heaven's Smile, Part 1, New York: Agni Press, 1974

LEARN TO LET GO

Often we place mental restrictions on people we love, whether it be parents "living their dreams" through their children, or someone "trapped" in a relationship. True love means loving people for who they are, not trying to channel them into who you want them to be. The greatest service you can do to one whom you love is allow them to grow into their soul's highest potential — sometimes this will mean actively helping them, but other times this will mean recognising when you are standing in the way of that happening and getting out of the way!

THE INNER STRENGTH: PATIENCE AND FORGIVENESS

> *Patience serves as a protection against wrong as clothes do against cold. For if you put on more clothes as the cold increases, it will have no power to hurt you .*[11]

To develop love, we also have to develop forgiveness and patience. To forgive someone, it helps to see beyond their surface imperfections and appreciate the beauty that lies deep within. Love always goes hand in hand with this recognition of inner beauty inside a person; it is recognising this deeper part of someone that helps bring it to the fore.

Developing this quality of love for everyone you meet allows you to rise above "the slings and arrows of outrageous fortune" and still keep your faith in humanity intact.

---

[11] Leonardo Da Vinci, The Notebooks of Leonardo da Vinci, English translation by Jean Paul Richter, 1888

DEALING WITH DIFFICULT PEOPLE

Life will always present us with awkward, difficult people; and unless you want to live in a Himalayan cave you will have to learn how to deal with such people. We should not let difficult individuals spoil our inner equanimity; with the right attitude we can maintain our peace of mind, even when dealing with unpleasant people. These are some suggestions for dealing with awkward people.

DON'T THINK ABOUT THEM ALL THE TIME

Sometimes when people cause us difficulties they start to dominate our thoughts; this makes their presence seem very close. However, it is best to think about them as little as possible. Instead, concentrate on things and people who inspire you. Thinking about difficult people is not going to change how they behave, but it will cause us unhappiness.

DON'T EXPECT TO CHANGE THEM

Awkward and unpleasant people are the least likely to be willing to change themselves. Don't take it upon yourself to try and change their behaviour; you will almost certainly fail. Furthermore, they will probably resent your interference and this will create further difficulties.

DON'T FEEL GUILTY

If people create problems in our life we can start to feel guilty, even though we have done nothing wrong. In cases like this we have to be detached; it may not be not our fault that problems have been created. As long as we seek to maintain a good attitude, that is all that matters.

SILENCE IS A POWERFUL WEAPON

When people say unreasonable things, the natural instinct is to try to argue with them. However, this draws us into their own particular perspective. In many circumstances, it may be appropriate to maintain silence and not respond to what they say and do. By being silent, we are effectively ignoring them without having to criticise their actions. In silence there is great power; when we ignore them, they lose influence. Silence also gives us time to think a more measured and detached response, for later.

RETAIN YOUR HUMOUR

Don't feel obliged to take every situation seriously. Try to see the funny side. If people behave in a ridiculous way, don't despair — just see the absurd behaviour as a humorous situation.

DON'T SEEK TO AVOID THEM

If you have to work with difficult people, the solution is rarely to move job. The likelihood is that you will find difficult people wherever you work. If you try to avoid difficult people, you will be permanently on the move. The thing to do is to change your attitude; rather than feeling depressed and guilty, we can see it is an opportunity for our self-improvement. Through learning to deal with difficulty people, we will learn many valuable life skills.

OFFER GOODWILL

If we can offer goodwill even to difficult people, we will make tremendous progress. Unpleasant people may deserve criticism, but this will not help the situation. Even the most difficult person may have one or two good qualities. Try to mentions these; subconsciously they will appreciate our goodwill. This remains the most effective way to bring out the best in others — even if it may seem to take a very long time.

BE KIND TO YOURSELF

We all know we should be kind to animals and considerate of other people, but are we actually kind to ourselves? If you regularly find that you are beating yourself up or are plagued by guilt, it is worth making an effort to be a bit kinder to yourself. Here are some ideas to help offer a bit of support for yourself.

THE PAST IS DUST

Past is Dust is one of the favourite sayings of my spiritual Teacher, Sri Chinmoy.

> *I always say the past is dust. By thinking of it and brooding over it we cannot change the past or free ourselves from guilt. If we have done something wrong, it is past. Let us think of the immediate future and allow it to grow into the immediacy of today.* .[12]

When we live in the past, we become plagued by regret and guilt. By constantly reliving the past, we cannot change what has gone before. If we have made mistakes in the past, we should not feel that this is our permanent reality. Focus instead on the present

---

[12] Sri Chinmoy, Inner Progress And Satisfaction-Life, New York: Agni Press, 1977

moment and see how you can improve and go forward. It is only by focusing on the present and doing the right thing that we can learn from the past.

DO ONE THING AT A TIME

We have all tried to juggle several things at once. We also know how stressful and difficult this is. Sometimes when we try to do several things at once, we give ourselves an exaggerated feeling of self-importance. However, don't pile pressure on yourself; value simplicity and do one thing at a time. When you focus on only your current activity, you are not only being kind to yourself, but also will be able to do things much more effectively.

GIVE TIME FOR YOUR SELF IMPROVEMENT

We spend many hours pleasing other people; 8 hours a day in the office, several hours meeting family and friends. Can we not find 15–20 minutes to look after ourselves? If we can find 20 minutes a day, we can learn how to relax, meditate and find a moment of calm in the rush of daily life. We may find, to our surprise, that this 20 minutes of quiet reflection makes us more productive and we don't actually lose any time at all.

DON'T CREATE UNNECESSARY PROBLEMS

Some problems are unavoidable and we have to deal with them with detachment and equanimity. However, if we are honest, some problems can easily be avoided. Do you really need to dispute with your colleagues about minor work issues?

DO NOT SEEK TO MEET THE EXPECTATIONS OF OTHERS

Some people can be quite demanding and place unrealistic expectations on us. Don't feel obliged to meet the expectations of others. If you try to please everyone, you will always be striving for an unattainable goal.

REMEMBER YOUR POSITIVE CONTRIBUTIONS

Sometimes our mistakes and faults stick in our mind more than the good things we have done. At the end of the day, take time to remember some of the constructive, positive things you have done. This does not have to be big achievements; sometimes a kind word to other people makes a big difference.

BE HAPPY

Life is there to be enjoyed. Don't feel that if you suffer you will make more progress. It is when we are happy and in a good consciousness that can we be of greatest service to others.

SELF ESTEEM

If you struggle with low self-esteem and feelings of inadequacy, these are some suggestions to gain self-confidence and increased self-esteem.

REMEMBER THE GOOD, FORGET THE BAD

If we are honest with ourselves, we will notice that we are all a mixture of bad qualities and good qualities. However, perhaps out of a sense of false modesty, we are more prone to remember our mistakes and weaknesses. It is this that makes us feel guilty and worthless, although we are doing ourselves a disservice. True, we have made some mistakes, but we have also done many good things. We should make a conscious effort to remember our good qualities and selfless actions for others. If we have made mistakes, we can learn from them, but we don't allow them to drag us down with feelings of guilt. Let go and move on.

DETACH FROM CRITICISM

You can't avoid getting criticised, but it is up to you whether you let it disturb your peace of mind. It is no one other than yourself who can rob you of inner peace. If you receive criticism, don't let it disturb your peace of mind. Feel it is criticising only an aspect of your character — an aspect you can easily improve.

If the criticism is unjust, pay no attention to it. Just leave it with the other person.

STOP PROCRASTINATING

Often feelings of inadequacy occur during periods of great procrastination. Rather than doing anything positive, we just think of all the things we haven't done. Here it is easy to get into a negative frame of mind — thinking of all the things we should be doing, but haven't. The cure for this is quite simple: stop procrastinating and start to achieve certain targets. As soon as we are actively working towards something we will have much greater self-confidence.

SET ACHIEVABLE GOALS

When we can have a feeling of achievement it is a great boost for our self-esteem. What we need to do is set small goals that enable us to have a feeling of self-improvement. We don't set unrealistic goals we will feel regret when we miss them. Our goals don't necessarily need to be material achievements. We can set inner targets of breaking bad habits or starting good habits.

LISTEN TO THE MIND LESS AND THE HEART MORE

The mind is full of judgemental thoughts about ourself and others. When we live in the mind we have a constant feelings of insecurity, doubt and pride. If we can identify with the qualities of our heart we will unmistakably feel improved self-esteem. This is because in the heart we can feel more easily our true sense of self.

KEEP FIT

The physical state of our body plays a crucial role in influencing our state of mind. If we are unfit and lethargic, it is like carrying a heavy weight around. Even if we try hard to ignore the body, it inevitably affects our state of mind and feelings of self-esteem. If you look after the body by keeping fit, you will feel better for exercising and doing something positive. Even if you are not particularly successful in losing weight, it is still worthwhile since you are making sincere attempts to improve your fitness. When we do nothing, either consciously or unconsciously we harbour feelings of inadequacy and guilt.

DON'T CRITICISE OTHERS

The human mind can be tricky at times. Quite often the mind tries to boost our self-esteem by criticising and denigrating others. The mind feels that if we point out the weaknesses of others we can feel somehow "superior" to others. This, however, is a false way to boost self-esteem. When we criticise other people, we are in a negative frame of mind and we are more likely to doubt ourselves. The thing to do is look for the best in others. If you try and boost other people's self esteem it will be much easier to increase your own self-esteem.

AVOID FEELINGS OF GUILT

Guilt does not help anyone. By cherishing feelings of guilt you cannot rescind your past actions. Make a resolution to avoid repeating the mistake, but then let go of your guilty feelings. Live in the present moment, not the past.

DRESS CONFIDENTLY

If you are immune to the opinion of the world, and care nothing for outer appearances you can dress like a street beggar and still have self-esteem. However, most of us do place great value on our physical appearance. This may be a sub conscious feeling, but if we dress in a confident and appropriate style we will be much more self-confident. One doesn't need to spend a fortune on clothes, but it is important to have the ability to dress in a way we are happy with.

DON'T BE A SLAVE TO HABITS

When we feel a slave to our own bad habits, we feel powerless to overcome them. This creates a strong feeling of regret and guilt. However, there is no rule that we have to be a victim of our own bad habits. Definitely, we can overcome our bad habits — just try concentrating on the right thing. This will enable us to break our bad habits.

MISUNDERSTANDINGS

It seems that in life, misunderstanding is easy to occur. Misunderstandings can create unnecessary conflict and unhappiness; often this results from a suspicious mind and unfairly assigning motives.

These are suggestions for preventing and resolving misunderstanding.

DON'T SUSPECT

Misunderstandings often arise because we suspect the worst. We may feel that someone has a negative attitude towards us, when actually they don't. The mind can be tricky, we can easily build up a negative image of someone; yet, it may be a false impression or at least only partially true. Often this stems from a lack of self-confidence. Because we doubt ourselves we assume that people are liable to be thinking badly about us. Another example is when we take lack of praise as a sign people think negatively of us. Just because someone doesn't offer praise outwardly, doesn't mean that they don't like us.

TALK HONESTLY

Most misunderstandings can be resolved by talking with other people. Meeting a person and talking over issues often shows that our
mind's imaginings were quite false. Be wary of communicating via
email; it is a very impersonal form of communication. There is no
body language and it is much easier to create misunderstandings.
Sometimes when we speak it is our facial expression and eyes that
offer the real meaning of what we are trying to convey.

USE THE HEART

The mind will always find conflict, problems and doubts. We need
to use the heart and concentrate on things which unite. Here the
heart is the aspect which does not judge or criticise but seeks oneness. Outwardly a person may create negative connotations; if this
is the case use the heart to silently concentrate on the inner qualities of the other person.

DON'T ASSIGN MOTIVES—YOU ARE PROBABLY WRONG

A common source of misunderstanding is assigning motives to other people. For example, someone may take a decision and then we
see it as a personal attack or personal criticism. Yet, we are often
100 percent incorrect in assigning this motive and assuming their
decision was taken to slight us. It can be very damaging to assume
others are out to get us. Often it is based on a "poor me" syndrome
— assuming the world is against us. If we cherish this negative
mindset, we will only succeed in making ourselves miserable. It
is also unfair to other people. When others suspect our motives,
we just feel disappointed that we have to try and convince others
our motives had nothing to do with their fears and suspicions. Of
course, sometimes people will act with ill feeling towards us; but,

we lose nothing by assuming people have a positive view. At the very least, we need to suspend our judgement and avoid jumping to conclusions.

KEEP PERSPECTIVE

Often we blow up small issues into big problems. Maybe someone we live with doesn't like the way we tidy up the house; but just because we get criticised for a small thing, doesn't mean they dislike us. We need to separate issues from personalities. Be prepared to accept small criticisms and not blow them out of proportion.

ASK—DON'T BROOD

Rather than brooding over misunderstanding, it is better to take action to resolve the situation. This may be through careful analysis of your thought patterns; you can resolve to detach from the negative thoughts you are currently holding. If you don't do this, if you ruminate over the same small misunderstandings, the mind will magnify the problem. What was once a small misunderstanding now feels to be a big misunderstanding. Try asking for clarification (in a non combative tone).

LOOK FOR RESOLUTIONS. DON'T CHERISH MISUNDERSTANDINGS AND INTRIGUE

If we cherish misunderstanding and intrigue, we will be inundated with them. We may do this only subconsciously, but if we seek to overcome them we will benefit from greater peace of mind and our relationships will definitely improve.

It is important to approach the problems in a non-combative way. If we challenge people and assign blame then they will be put on the defensive.

If we approach others with a non-judgemental attitude, it makes it much easier for others to respond in a positive way.

BE WARY OF GOSSIP. TAKE TIME TO FIND OUT THE TRUTH

This advice may seem obvious, but it is nevertheless something worth reminding ourselves of. In the world there is much criticism, some true, but some false. We can't assume that something we hear or see is necessarily true. We need to find out for ourselves and use our common sense and judgement. If we wholeheartedly believe second-hand sources, we risk creating needless misunderstandings.

SELF CRITICISM
AND SELF ENCOURAGEMENT

Do you want to be always happy?
Then give up fighting
For negativity
And learn the beautiful art
Of self-encouragement.[13]

It is a fine balance between self-encouragement and self-criticism. To honestly evaluate ourselves is a difficult task. We tend to either conveniently ignore our own faults or become too harsh on ourselves for small inconsequential things. We need a balance of self-encouragement and honest self-appraisal; getting the right balance is not so easy.

DON'T BE ASHAMED OF YOUR FAULTS

If we can't be honest with ourself, who can we be honest with? The mind can be good at justifying our wrong actions and behaviour, but clever self-justification is of no benefit in the long run. If we can be aware of our own pride, jealousy and insecurities, then we have a chance to let go of them. But, if we always justify our wrong attitudes to ourself then we are lost.

---

[13] Sri Chinmoy, Ten Thousand Flower-Flames, Part 12, #1120. New York: Agni Press, 1981

AVOID GUILT

One of the reasons we may seek to ignore our faults is that we feel guilty. To avoid feeling guilty we avoid criticising ourself. However, it is better to be self-critical without feelings of guilt. Guilt is an emotion that doesn't help but makes us feel more inadequate. Become aware of what you want to change and see it as a positive movement.

> *Not self-contempt*
> *But self-improvement*
> *Has to be our continuous choice.*[14]

DON'T JUDGE BY THE VALUES OF OTHERS

The biggest problem here is that we start to judge ourselves by the standards of others. Our friends may have been put out because of something we did; therefore, they try to make us feel guilty. Since others are critical of us, we feel obliged to feel guilty too.

In actual fact, we need to be firm and reject others' criticisms — if they are not justified. In the eyes of the world we may have done something wrong, but only we ourselves know our inner attitude. We may have done something with the best of intentions and motivations, but because of circumstances beyond our control things turned out badly. The world may criticise us, but we know we did our best. How can we criticise ourselves for bad luck or circumstances beyond our control? On the other hand, we may get praise when we don't deserve it.

Also, although we shouldn't accept the misinformed criticism of others, we should be open to the suggestions of others. Often

---

[14] Sri Chinmoy, Sri Chinmoy Seventy-Seven Thousand Service-Trees, Part 19, #18362. New York: Agni Press, 2000

people can see things about ourselves that we can't. Don't be too proud to take advice / suggestions / criticism from others. It is not a sign of weakness to listen to other people. Our sincerity will know whether they are telling the truth or not.

JUDGE MOTIVES RATHER THAN OUTCOME

As mentioned in the previous point it is our inner attitude which is important. A small action done selflessly without expectation of reward is worth more than some egoistic actions which may appear to have a better outcome. It is our inner attitude that we need to be aware of.

REMAIN BALANCED

When we start to criticise ourself it is easy to lose a sense of proportion and start beating ourselves up over a small issue. This is a real mistake. We might make small mistakes but making them into big problems just makes the situation worse. Never lose a sense of proportion and don't magnify small problems. At the same time don't be dismissive of actions that are causing pain to others.

SELF CRITICISM AND SELF ENCOURAGEMENT

Focusing on the negative doesn't help. The most effective self-criticism is to also learn the art of self-encouragement. Be aware of the good selfless deeds and thoughts you have and give these more importance. If we strengthen our good qualities then this will take care of most of our weaknesses. The positive approach is by far the best way to help our self-improvement.

DIFFERENT TYPES OF PEOPLE

People are a mixture of qualities and personalities. At various times, we all embody these different aspects and qualities. But often some quality or trait is more predominant than others. Some friends will be insecure and shy; others will be brash and egocentric. We need to respond to these different characteristics in different ways. There are also some general tips for dealing with difficult people here.

Dealing with difficult people is certainly one of the most important life skills and as painful as it may be, it can be very instructive. Even if it is just learning — don't be like them!

EGOCENTRIC PEOPLE

An egocentric person tends to talk a lot — usually about themselves and their achievements, they look for compliments and so will often compliment others to encourage praise for themselves. They dislike any criticism and are often insecure, though they hide this insecurity by trying to display their successes. Egocentric people can be a bit of a bore, but it will not help to point out their shortcomings, as they will not appreciate your intervention. It is best to offer sincere praise if justified, but not to encourage them excessively. If they really are talking too much about themselves, politely but firmly steer the conversations onto something else.

Very insecure and egocentric people will try to put down other people to make themselves feel better. This is pretty frustrating but, before taking it personally, it is worth being aware of why they are doing it so don't take it to heart.

There is a saying "pride comes before a fall." If you feel someone's ego is ballooning out of control, don't despair or worry too much. Sooner or later they are sowing their own downfall.

OPINIONATED PEOPLE

Opinionated people have strongly-held views and tend to be quite confrontational. Whatever the issue is — the price of bread, the best place to put the flower pot, the cause of the credit crunch — you can guarantee they will have a strong opinion and they will vigorously argue their point of view and won't be particularly interested in anyone else's opinion. On many issues you can side-step them. After all, there are few things in life really worth arguing about — so just avoid bringing up the topics that they will give their interminable lectures on. It is also worth remembering you are probably not going to be able to change their mind.

The problem comes when they have a strongly held opinion on something which is important and that you can't simply ignore. This maybe an issue that affects you or people around you. It is difficult because they are usually quite set in their ways.

The best tactic is not to challenge them head on. Don't start by saying "I think you are wrong," as they will resent this direct challenge. Try looking for some area of agreement and consensus; get them in a good frame of mind and then suggest an improvement or different way of doing things. There is, however, no one particular way of dealing with this issue. Sometimes, we just have to be firm. Just because someone is opinionated and will throw a tantrum if they don't get their way doesn't mean we have to give in to them. Never feel guilty for standing up to some behaviour that is wrong, but where possible make it as least confrontational as possible.

SHY / INSECURE PEOPLE

Someone who is shy and insecure will be reluctant to come forward; they will lack confidence and often try hard to please people, even if inwardly they regret doing this. It is important to bear in mind that shy people will need encouragement and support. Small steps to boost their confidence will make a big difference. Don't be patronising but give people the opportunity to speak and be true to themselves. Shy people are often quite self-critical so there is little need to make a big deal out of criticising small misdemeanours. The main thing is that they will respond positively to even small amounts of encouragement.

LAZY PEOPLE

Lazy people don't create so many problems, but laziness can become selfishness when you have to do their work for them. Try giving them a sense of duty and make them aware of how they impact on other people. They might not change for themselves, but they may become less lazy when they realise others have to carry the can.

LOVING DIFFICULT PEOPLE

It is easy to love people we like, but more challenging to love difficult and awkward people. The nature of real love is that it encom-
passes all. Love should not be self-serving — and in loving difficult
people we learn its real meaning. In the words of Shakespeare:

> ....*Love is not love*
> *Which alters when it alteration finds,*
> *Or Bends with the remover to remove.*
> *O, no! It is an ever-fixed mark,*
> *That looks on tempests and is never shaken.*
> *It is the star to every wandering bark,*
> *Whose worth's unknown, although his height be taken.*[15]

But how to love difficult people?

LOOK BEYOND DEFECTS

Feel that a person's defects and weaknesses are only a partial reflec
tion of his/her real nature. Feel that behind their exterior personality there is their real self, trying to break through. Often difficult
people are seeking attention / love in irritating ways. They are like
a child struggling to know what the right thing to do is. We don't

---

[15] Shakespeare, William, Sonnet 116, 1609

have to love their weaknesses; we are trying to love the true self, hidden underneath.

OUR PEACE OF MIND

Other people may give us reason to dislike them; we may even start hating them, but what do we gain by hating others? When we hate or condemn others we lose something precious in ourselves. When we judge others, it is often because we have that quality within ourselves.

> *Hate is often an obverse form of love.*
> *You hate someone whom you really wish to love but whom*
> *you cannot love .*[16]

When we love others without judgement it brings our own best qualities to the fore. If we love others, if we seek to see the good — even in difficult people — we will benefit tremendously and gain peace of mind. It is one of the great paradoxes — by loving unselfishly and unconditionally we benefit ourselves.

LOVE DOES NOT MEAN ACQUIESCENCE

We can love people without agreeing with their bad behaviour. Nor do we have to agree with their demands and unreasonable expectations. Because a mother loves her child, the mother will reprimand the child when he places himself in danger. We can love a person whilst at the same time discouraging them from behaving badly. We can love the person whilst at the same time disliking some things they do.

---

[16] Sri Chinmoy, Earth's Cry Meets Heaven's Smile, Part 3, New York: Agni Press, 1978

EMPATHY

In their own way people are trying to do the right thing. At times, it may not feel like it; however, we can gain a lot through sympathetic understanding. We can try to feel that the mistakes they are making are ones that we ourselves have made at various times. When there is a feeling of superiority there is no real love and oneness, but if we can feel the other person as part of ourself then we will naturally have good will towards them. It is this ability to identify with others which enables a real feeling of love to develop.

DON'T EXPECT TO CHANGE THEM

If we feel responsible for changing those whom we love, we will always be doomed to disappointment. Even our own kith and kin are responsible for their own lives. The biggest obstacle to loving difficult people is to think "I will love them, but they have to become better people first." If we wait for people to become better before loving, then we will be doomed to disappointment. It is because people are imperfect that they need our compassion and understanding. If we can accept people as they are, then even difficult people we can appreciate.

PART IV

LIFE

KEEPING THINGS IN PERSPECTIVE

A sense of perspective is vital to keeping sane, and avoiding small problems that can unnecessarily overwhelm us. If we lose perspective we can end up worrying for hours about things that may never even happen. To keep things in perspective it is particularly important to live in the present moment and avoid being overwhelmed by fears and concerns about the future.

Here are some tips to keep things in a sense of perspective.

SEE THINGS FROM OTHER PEOPLE'S POINT OF VIEW

This is something that can be quite difficult to do. When you feel aggrieved at a situation or person, try to place yourself in their shoes and try to understand their motivations and actions. We don't necessarily have to agree and sympathise with them, but if we can really see an issue from other people's perspective, we can sincerely understand a very different view of the issue. This will help us be more sympathetic in our judgement and response.

DOES IT MATTER WHAT OTHER PEOPLE THINK?

If someone makes a critical judgement, don't let it be the end of your world. Just because we have received some negative feedback, it doesn't mean it is entirely true or that we should take it to heart. Criticism invariably results from some small mistake; and doesn't reflect on our overall character.

ARE YOU MISJUDGING OTHER PEOPLE?

Sometimes problems occur because we wrongly assume other people are acting from a particular motivation. The mind suspects and assumes the worst, yet often we may be incorrect in our assumptions. If someone fails to acknowledge our presence or contribution, we should avoid making the jump to assuming that they therefore no longer like us. The mind can be very tricky — it can take a small incident and magnify it out of all proportion. It is important to be very careful in judging people's motives, especially when we assume them to be negative. If we suspect the worst we lose something precious within us.

DOES THIS CAUSE ANY MAJOR PROBLEMS?

Sometimes we can get worked up about problems that are very insignificant. Perhaps we like to keep things in a certain order, but our house companions fail to clean up. It's a bit inconvenient if people leave dirty washing in the sink, but at the same time it's not the end of the world. Think about the things that have concerned you in the past few days and be honest in questioning how important they really are.

DETACH FROM THE MIND

Our thoughts are not always reliable. It is important to be able to evaluate our own thoughts and decide whether or not they are accurate. Sometimes when we wake up in the morning we have a different perspective on yesterdays problems. The reason is that during sleep the mind switches off temporarily. Therefore, the new day can often give a fresh, more optimistic perspective. However, we don't have to wait until we sleep for 8 hours to switch off from the mind. Through learning meditation and how to control our thoughts, we can still the mind even during waking hours. If we cultivate this inner silence, it helps to evaluate issues from a higher perspective. Meditation enhances our capacity to look at issues with our intuitive capacity and not just the intellectual mind.

ASK A THIRD PARTY FOR THEIR VIEWS

It is said that those who need advice are those most unwilling to be receptive to any advice. However, asking others can be beneficial for seeing another perspective. It is important that we not only ask others, but are willing to take their views on board. It is also important to ask the right person; someone who doesn't have a vested interest or have prejudged the issues

BE WILLING TO THINK YOU MAY BE WRONG

Our initial judgements are often wrong. It is a mistake to hold onto these views rigidly. Our perspective is more likely to be inaccurate and unbalanced when we become deeply attached to a particular outlook. Sometimes our pride and ego can make us reluctant to soften or alter our perspective. Our ego can exaggerate our problems and blow things up out of proportion.

CONCENTRATE ON GOOD THINGS

Another thing we can try is just to ignore the problem / issue completely and throw ourselves into something different. Absorbing ourselves in another task allows time to ignore the problem. Later we realise that what seemed like a big problem before, is now less problematic.

OBSERVATIONS ON LIFE

A few thoughts on life.
- It is easy to see the faults in others, but how many people are willing to admit their own faults and limitations?
- We rarely regret being kind and sympathetic to others.
- Money cannot guarantee us happiness, but neither can poverty. Happiness requires a detachment from both financial worries and a desire for endless riches.
- We spend hours at school learning calculus and other useless subjects; we spend hours learning to drive a car and how to fill in tax forms. Why can't we spend a few minutes learning how to control our own mind?
- The fulfilment of a desire rarely brings peace; usually new desires take their place.
- If we avoid a problem, we usually find the problem reoccurs in a different set of circumstances. No matter how hard we try to avoid it, eventually we have to face up to the problem.
- "We are all in the gutter, but some of us are looking at the stars" — Oscar Wilde. To some people the world is a depressing and ugly place; to others the world is beautiful and full of hope. It is all a matter of choice.

- Real relaxation does not just involve sitting in a comfy chair. Relaxation requires us to switch off from our overactive mind.
- Brooding over problems invariably makes them worse. There is a lot to be said for just forgetting them.
- What you think about will, in some form, come into your life. Be careful what you wish for.
- In the mad rush of modern life, there is great peace to be found in spending 30 minutes in quiet reflection.
- Worries and anxieties rarely materialise and when they do, they are usually less problematic than we feared.
- Anger is a quick poison. It's main effect is to make us miserable and lose our sense of perspective.
- Poise is a beautiful quality. The best cure for nervousness and worry is the cultivation of calmness, detachment and inner poise.
- Sometimes we do things we know are wrong, but we can't stop ourselves. The burnt hand strengthens our conscience more than we might admit.
- Why should we be at peace just at odd times in the day? The greatest challenge in life is to maintain inner peace and inner equanimity throughout the day; it is the best way to be happy even during the most testing experiences.
- A truth doesn't cease to be truth, just because it is unpopular.
- Although it is easy to judge but more difficult to forgive, each person is trying in their own way to do the right thing.
- Constant noise is not necessary. A person who cannot spend time on his own is ill at ease with himself and the world.
- To have great enthusiasm for an activity is a real blessing. When we are motivated and enthusiastic we can do unimaginable things.

o How can we find our goal, if we never think about it? It is all too easy to be lost in an endless rush of activity and busyness, forgetting the important things in life.

o We might not welcome adversity into our lives, but difficult situations can bring about a beneficial transformation that would never have occurred otherwise.

o A moment of sincere gratitude does help us appreciate the finer things of life.

o Cynicism may have various justifications, but constant cynicism and mistrust will never change the world and will certainly never bring peace of mind or happiness.

o We should never feel worthless because everyone, in some way, has the capacity to inspire others.

o Alas, we are often too reluctant to offer a kind thought and kind words.

o Remaining silent when you are tempted to argue and vent your frustrations can save you on many occasions.

o Write down a list of worries and anxieties that have gone through your mind during the day. If we are honest, we will be a bit embarrassed at how pathetic and unrealistic some of them are.

o Smiling really is the easiest and cheapest way to make yourself and others happy.

o To sincerely admire other people is to feel a oneness with their good qualities. It can definitely help us to make these qualities part of ourselves.

- Trying to convince people through argument and debate is as futile as asking the broken computer to kindly start working again.
- It may be hard to believe, but life really did exist before the invention of cars, mobile phones, email and instant messaging; apparently, people were even quite happy.
- We absorb from others by osmosis. Whomever we spend time with will affect our state of mind — whether for better or worse.
- Music has a unique capacity to inspire, soothe and uplift the soul. If we have no time for music, what are we doing with our life?
- Perfect, selfless love is very rare in this world.
- Jealousy of others' success is to make ourselves needlessly miserable.
- There is nothing worse than depression. Depression has to be fought with every ounce of our inner strength.
- We tend to think of Hollywood stars as having glittering lives. But, why do so many end up with broken relationships and mental problems? They are only successful in pursuit of a pseudo happiness — the fleeting pleasures of name and fame.
- Silence is a much underrated quality in modern life.
- People who try to dominate others invariably are full of insecurities.

OLD AGE

Many people, including the retired themselves, see old age in a negative way. They see their declining physical abilities as a reason to draw back and retire from many activities they used to enjoy. However, there is no reason why old age cannot give us as much inspiration, enjoyment and newness as our formative younger years. Perhaps they can be even better, as we have the benefit of experience.

DO NOT GIVE UP

It is true that in old age our faculties will not be as good. Our hearing, eyesight etc. will be a little diminished. Yet, even though we may be a little slower than before, this is no reason to stop doing things that we used to enjoy. The first thing we should do is not to compare ourselves by the same standards as in the prime of our youth. If we are a keen runner, for example, our times will invariably slow down compared to our youth. However, we should not feel bad about slower times. Rather than comparing to 20 years ago, we should seek to do a seasonal best each year. What is important is that we get a good feeling from our running or other activity.

YOUNG AT HEART

Old age is as much a state of mind as it is a physical deterioration. By our attitude we may feel old at the age of 40; by the same token a 90 year old can feel young at heart. If we constantly think about age as a barrier then we allow the negative effects of old age to influence our mind. However, if we do not place importance on age, we can look on the world with the eyes of a young person. To be able to do this, we should live in the heart and not in the critical mind. The nature of the mind is to welcome negative, restricting thoughts. It is the mind which will over-exaggerate the importance of physical age. If we live in the heart we remain at the source of spontaneity and newness.

STUCK IN A GROOVE

Old people are more likely to get stuck in a groove, following the same routine. This routine can become constricting and limits our potentials for discovering joy in new activities. Again it mainly depends on our mental attitude. Just because we are old, we should not feel the necessity of doing the same thing every day. There is no reason why in old age we cannot start new activities. interestingly, both Tagore and Churchill began painting in the evening of their life.

If you are approaching your more mature years, do not despair and give up; seek to enjoy life to the full and remain young at heart and see in how many ways you can try to do new, inspiring activities. You will definitely inspire others.

SMALL THINGS THAT
CAN MAKE A BIG DIFFERENCE

When we wish to improve our life we assume we need to make radical changes. We look for some programme or person who will fundamentally change our life. However, with this attitude we forget that we can radically change our life just by making a few small changes.

Try these suggestions and consider what impact they have on your life.

BE PATIENT

When you are standing in a line waiting for slow customer service, instead of getting frustrated see this as an opportunity to remain calm and peaceful. Many people regularly get upset and angry because of small defects in the quality of a good service. However, becoming upset does not help in any way; all you do is to try and spread your unhappiness. The next time you are victim to an unavoidable delay, don't lose your equanimity but be patient. If you can retain peace of mind in these situations you life will benefit immeasurably. All we are trying to do is change our habitual response and perspective to these unavoidable events.

SMILE

A smile costs nothing, but it creates a powerful positive vibration. When we smile we are offering our good will to the other person. Furthermore, this good will is much more effective than anything we can say. We should not just smile at our friends, but also at those who cause us consternation. If our smile is sincere it can remove many negative feelings and defuse tense situations. People will unconsciously respond positively to us when we smile. Whatever the situation, smiling will help. Research also suggests that smiling helps us.

> Smile, my heart, smile.
> Your smile means so much to me,
> Your smile feeds my reality within,
> Your smile liberates me from world-clamour and
>   world-din.
> Smile, my heart, smile.
> Smile at least once in a while.[17]

OFFER GRATITUDE

It only takes a moment, but if we appreciate the efforts / presence of other people, it will create much goodwill. Our gratitude does not have to be an ostentatious display of affection. It may merely be recognition of someone's efforts.

To recognise someone's efforts is, in a way, to offer gratitude to that person. In particular, try to offer gratitude to people who are working without demanding immediate recognition.

---

[17] Sri Chinmoy, A Soulful Cry Versus A Fruitful Smile, New York: Agni Press, 1977

Offering gratitude also helps us; by appreciating the good qualities of others we help to make these part of ourselves. Gratitude is therefore a powerful antidote to developing jealousy.

DON'T DO TWO THINGS AT ONCE

Quite often I try to do several things at once, especially when I have my computer turned on. However, when I concentrate on only one thing at a time, it is much more effective and powerful. Doing one thing at a time enables great focus and it relieves us of much tension. Whatever we do, we should try to give it our undivided attention. When eating food, don't try to read the newspaper as well. When speaking to a friend, don't be thinking of a work problem. By concentrating on only thing we will do things quicker and better.

DO SOMETHING GOOD WITHOUT DEMANDING RECOGNITION

It is easy to do one good deed in the day, however we also feel that this deed deserves recognition and praise. If we can work without demanding recognition, people will eventually appreciate our selfless service. More importantly, we are then acting with the best selfless motives and through this we can make tremendous progress and gain inner peace.

AVOID GOSSIP AND SAY SOMETHING POSITIVE

If people at work or at home are criticising somebody, go against the prevailing mood and find something positive to say about the person. Even if this person deserves to be criticised, it does not help to magnify his negative qualities. If you can find something positive to say, it will help immensely.

REMOVE ONE DESIRE FROM YOUR ENDLESS LIST

At any one point in time, we have countless desires for material things and for outer recognition. Try making a list and then cross off at least one of these desires. If we can reduce our desires and expectations, we can learn to appreciate that happiness does not depend on the fulfilment of desire.

POSITIVE THINKING

We often hear the mantra that positive thinking is a key to our success and happiness. It is true that thoughts are of crucial importance in shaping experiences in our life. But, what do we actually mean by positive thinking? When is positive thinking helpful and when is it a hindrance?

WHAT POSITIVE THINKING IS NOT

EXPECTING THAT THOUGHTS ALONE CAN BRING SUCCESS

Good thoughts are important for success, but Edmund Hilary didn't climb Mount Everest just by thinking about it. Combine positive thinking by taking practical steps. Don't just dream — act.

IGNORING OUR WEAKNESSES

We need to develop self-confidence and belief in our capacities, but this should not be mistaken for pride and arrogance. If we feel that we are always right, this is a real mistake. This is not so much positive thinking as arrogant wishful thinking. We need to combine self-confidence with a quiet humility.

EXPECTING PEOPLE WILL BEHAVE IN A CERTAIN WAY

Positive thinking should not assume that we could change someone's nature just through positive thoughts. We should avoid magnifying people's weaknesses, but it is a mistake to feel that we can change someone's nature through positive thinking. In practise we will always be disappointed. Positive thinking can be used to offer goodwill to others, but do not expect fundamental change from others.

DESIRE FOR GREAT RICHES THROUGH POSITIVE THINKING

George Bernard Shaw said there are two tragedies in life "One is to lose your heart's desire. The other is to gain it." We may feel that positive thinking is, for example repeating a mantra like "I will be rich, I will have loads of money." We may indeed get money, but is this what will give us abiding satisfaction? Positive thinking should be used for our self-improvement and not our self aggrandisement.

HOW POSITIVE THINKING CAN BENEFIT

HAVE CONFIDENCE IN YOURSELF

If we don't have self-confidence, we will never fulfil our potential. Self-confidence means we avoid filling our mind with negative thoughts and doubts. It means we have faith in our capacities. It also means that we are happy to be who we are, and not try to be somebody else.

SEEING THE BEST IN OTHERS

It is easy to see the faults in other people. Often a person's faults are their most memorable qualities. However, we should try to bring to the fore the good qualities inherent in other people. This is the best way to bring out the best in others. If we concentrate on their weaknesses they just resent it. Here positive thinking is very helpful, because it helps us be more tolerant and understanding.

Only by our positive thinking,
By our bringing the positive qualities
Of others to the fore,
Will this world be able
To make progress.[18]

DON'T BE SUSPICIOUS

We live in a suspicious world, but if we always assume that people are acting from the worst motives, we lose something precious in ourselves. There is an old saying: "A Saint sees everyone else as a saint, a thief looks upon everyone else as a thief." How we view the world is, to some extent, a reflection of ourself. Therefore, we should not project our suspicions onto other people, but instead be non judgemental. This does not mean we have a blind trust in others. It means we don't automatically assume a critical mindset. Let us give people the benefit of the doubt; if we are disappointed later, no harm.

GRATITUDE

Gratitude is a wonderful quality which enables us to appreciate the good and beautiful. If we have gratitude we will develop a positive feeling for the world. Gratitude is more than positive thinking; gratitude is our sincere appreciation for other people and other things. It is through gratitude that we can easily avoid a negative frame of mind.

---

[18] Sri Chinmoy, Seventy-Seven Thousand Service-Trees, Part 15, #14779. New York: Agni Press, 1999

A SILENT MIND

A silent mind creates a very positive vibration. We don't always need to fill our mind with lots of so-called "positive thoughts" When we cultivate a silent mind, we develop inner peace, which is a very powerful quality. A silent mind enables us to gain focus and an inner inspiration. Therefore, we should take time to silence the mind for a certain period every day. We will find after a period of meditation, positive thinking comes naturally, it doesn't have to be forced.

SUCCESS

What is success and how can we achieve it?

SUCCESS AND HAPPINESS

Does success leave you feeling satisfied and sincerely happy, or does it just leave you just striving for more? Some people have difficulty enjoying success because whatever they achieve is not enough. It is like fulfilling one desire, only to have two more take its place. We have to learn to enjoy our success. If we cannot be at peace with ourselves is it really success?

WORKING WITH OTHERS

> *No man*
> *Is an island.*[19]

If we seek to succeed on our own, we cut ourselves off from the support and guidance of others. Often when we try to succeed on our own we bring to the fore our pride and ego; there is a feeling of self-sufficiency that makes us unwilling to take the necessary help of others. We need to feel that success is not just about ourselves, but a team effort. Even if one person succeeds in rowing solo across the Atlantic, they will feel some appreciation for their

---

[19] John Donne

trainer, and the mechanic who helped prepare for the task. It is not possible to do everything on your own. If you feel oneness with others you will gain more happiness from your success. If you try to keep all the success just for yourself, you limit your possibilities.

VISION

To succeed we need to have a clear vision of what we wish to achieve; it is important to keep these aspirations in the forefront of our mind. We need to have a clarity of purpose and intent that will keep us focused. It is this belief and vision that will prevent us from being discouraged by critics and naysayers. The world can be a negative place; it is easier to disbelieve and criticise than it is to encourage people of vision. If you want to succeed and achieve something new, there will be an inevitable resistance from some parts of society. Success depends on a clarity of focus which prevents you being deterred and held back by others.

THE EGO AND SUCCESS

What is our motivation behind our success? Is it to prove ourselves superior or is it to offer something worthwhile to others? If we are motivated only by a desire to inflate our ego, success can only be of a limited nature. Real success is about achieving something worthwhile; it should be something that others can feel part of. The greatest success may be to work completely in the background without others knowing.

SELF TRANSCENDENCE

Success often conjures up ideas of trophies, gaining money, power and prestige. But, why does success have to be synonymous with "winning" something. Success can be measured in our continual progress, and transcendence of previous limitations. When we succeed in this way, success is an on going process, it is not just limited to the completion of a certain task. Sometimes when we achieve something, we feel we have succeeded, but then we relax and stop making any forward progress. Real success is continual progress, not just a fixed point in time.

SUCCESS AND FAILURE

Success and failure are the two sides of the same coin. Failure is intrinsic to our success. If we can look upon failure as a stepping-stone to progress, we will not get discouraged. A successful person has many failures, it is just that they are able to learn from them and move on. Don't blame fate but see it as a necessary experience.

> *What is failure? Failure is an experience which awakens us. What is success? Success is an experience which energises us to strive for a higher and greater success. And what is progress? Progress is an experience which illumines us and fulfils us .[20]*

---

[20] Sri Chinmoy, Fifty Freedom-Boats To One Golden Shore, Part 2, New York: Agni Press, 1974

DETERMINATION AND PERSISTENCE

Success requires persistence. Modern society perhaps encourages us to expect instant results and instant fixes, but the secret of success lies in persistence. "Never give up" should be our motto. There are always reasons to be discouraged, but we have to be willing to persist and go on.

COULD YOU DO THIS?

Sometimes it is good to look at life from a different perspective and offer ourselves challenges. Challenges don't have to be physical challenges like running a marathon or climbing a mountain. Setting personal challenges test our inner attitude to life; it tests how much we hang onto our ego and how much we can be liberated from the confines of the mind. They are not necessarily easy to do, but it is an interesting experience and offers a different perspective on life.

COULD YOU GET JOY FROM YOUR ENEMY'S ACHIEVEMENT?

Think of a person that you dislike or someone who just irritates you. Suppose that they did something really great for the world, how would you feel? Would you be happy and proud they had at last done something good? Or would you be unable to offer appreciation, feeling a mixture of jealousy and pride that you are still better than them. If we can appreciate people who have irritated us, it means we have a magnanimous heart. It means we can detach from insignificant problems and worries. Too often we allow certain things to permanently cloud our judgement and opinion of others.

FEEL GRATEFUL FOR CRITICISM

We like praise; we dislike criticism. This is an instinctive view of life. However, it is often very difficult to receive criticism in the right way. The problem is that when criticised we feel personally offended, even though the criticism maybe over a small action. The criticism may be unjustified, or it may be spot on. Even if criticism is offered with unkind words, it can still contain very good advice which can help us improve. If we just took criticism as an opportunity to learn and grow, we could look upon criticism as beneficial as praise. In fact criticism maybe more useful than praise; we learn little from praise, but it does boost the ego.

WORK ENTIRELY WITHOUT RECOGNITION

Could we work really hard without any desire or need for recognition and appreciation? Quite often we might serve others, but there is some condition attached to our service. In particular, we expect to have some kind of recognition and reward. Often we may do something with genuinely selfless motives; we act from the heart because we feel it is the right thing to do. However, at a later stage the mind comes to the fore demanding recognition or feels slighted because we haven't been praised to the skies. It is as if we have a split personality. Part of us is happy to be unnoticed, but another part spoils everything by being distressed at a lack of recognition. To work entirely selflessly means we are working for a sincere cause and not for our human ego

KEEP THE MIND PERFECTLY SILENT FOR THREE MINUTES

Man has conquered space; man has conquered Everest. But how many people have conquered their own mind — which should, in theory, be the easiest thing to control? Try sitting quiet and still and then observe the thoughts going through your mind. Then try to stop all thoughts, try to think of absolutely nothing — just concentrate on your breathing. If you can have an absolutely still mind for 3 minutes then you will make very good progress with meditation; it will be an invaluable tool for cultivating inner peace. (By the way, falling asleep for 3 minutes does not count as meditation — although it is one way to quieten the mind....) However, you may also find it is really quite difficult to control your mind. This seems to be a paradox, since if it is our mind and we can decide, why is it so difficult to calm and to be at our command?

SPEND A DAY WITHOUT CRITICISING ANYBODY

The world has plenty of critics, there are countless justifications for complaining about X,Y,Z; but could you spend a day without criticising your friends, family and work colleagues? Here, we should avoid criticising on an inner plane as well as with words. It is difficult to avoid gossiping about people, but to keep our thoughts clear of gossip is even more difficult.

DIFFICULT THINGS TO DO

We aspire to do many things, but for some reason they remain quite difficult. It is better to have the right intention and be aware of how difficult they are. These are some of the things that are very difficult to do and how we could make them a little more practical.

ADMIT WE'RE WRONG

Nearly all of us find it difficult to admit we were wrong. It stems from a false belief that we somehow always expect ourselves to be right. Part of the problem is our pride. We feel embarrassed to admit we get things wrong; we feel it somehow diminishes our own standing. But, to admit we were wrong is a sign of strength, flexibility and humility. People will never think ill of us simply because we admit to making a mistake. The mind's insistence on trying to justify everything we do merely creates problems for others and ourselves. We need to change our mindset and be happy to admit to mistakes without feelings of guilt or humbled pride.

BE NON JUDGEMENTAL

We come across many people in life; some we like, some we dislike. Our mind is constantly judging people, on their appearance or on what they say. Consequently, our interactions with them are clouded by our judgement. It is much better to have a clear mind without prejudging others.

ACCEPT CRITICISM IN GOOD SPIRIT

Criticism can be an excellent opportunity to learn and develop. Without criticism we may continue to make mistakes and gain a large ego. Yet, despite the benefits of receiving constructive criticism, we feel challenged and personally affronted. We love to receive praise but struggle to deal with criticism.

BE CHEERFUL UNDER ALL CIRCUMSTANCES

Life presents us with ups and downs, whether we like it or not. There is nothing we can do about our circumstances and sometimes fate gives us challenging circumstances. Becoming miserable does not help; it only makes the situation more difficult. To remain cheerful in difficult circumstances is a great boon. Cheerfulness can overcome many obstacles and help us to discover light even in seemingly difficult times. Unfortunately, when things don't go to plan, we start feeling sorry for ourselves and feel glum. Of course this does not help, but this is what we tend to do.

PRACTISE WHAT WE PREACH

Alas, it is easy to say what we should do, but it is another thing to do it! If world peace could be attained by good intentions it would have been achieved a long time ago. Quite often we know what we should do, we hear our voice of conscience or message from our heart, but some other force prevents us from doing the right thing. Even worse, we tell others what to do — when we have no intention of doing it ourselves. Still, to have good intentions is a start. What we need to do is talk a little less and act a little more. Putting into effect our good intentions is the real challenge.

LISTEN

Everyone wants to talk, but how many have time to listen? Listening is a great art. Just listening to others can help them to work out their problems. They don't need our advice, but they may need an opportunity to work out what they should do. If you dominate conversations and always like to have the last word, sit back and try to listen, especially to those who are shy or need a reliable friend.

DO ONE THING AT A TIME

Simplicity and focus are great virtues, but we feel if we can try to do two things at once we will get more done. Alas, this rarely works; we just get stressed from the demands we place on ourselves, stress that need not be there.

GET UP EARLY IN THE MORNING

How beautiful it is to get up at dawn, listening to the dawn chorus before the rush of humanity enters the day.

NO COMPLAINTS

A while back, when I tried a period of not criticising people, it was an interesting experiment, if rather difficult. In a similar vein I thought it would be interesting to see what life is like if we make zero complaints about anything.

We tend to be chronic complainers. We complain about other people, about our work situation, about what is on the telly, the fact Gas prices have risen 15%; we complain about what is happening in our life, in our house and around the world. There seems to be no end in sight to our long list of complaints. Living without complaining is not burying our head in the sand thinking the world has no problems. The crucial question is — what does complaining achieve? How does constant complaining affect our own life? Does complaining about things we have no control over help in any way?

YOU CAN'T CHANGE THE WORLD BUT YOU CAN CHANGE YOURSELF

The road to inner peace is never dependent on ironing out all the problems of society and the world first. Governments will always be making bad decisions, buses will always be arriving late, and electronic devices will always be breaking down.

If we write down what we most like to complain about, these will probably not change. Some people think that if only they could move country all their complaints would vanish; but this is wishful thinking. The problems will be there in other countries, just in other forms. The important thing is to change our attitude. Rather than complain, we can try to tolerate the mistakes of others; rather than complain over silly things, we can maintain an attitude of detachment.

We need to love and accept the world as it is. We cannot wait for the world to be perfect before we love. The important thing is to be positive — looking for the good rather than looking for legitimate complaints.

COMPLAINING VERSUS GRATITUDE

When we complain we look for the negative. We give power to our negative thoughts and the world seems a darker place. If we look for the positive, if we aspire to cultivate gratitude for the good in life — our outlook will completely change. We will give power, focus and attention to the good and beautiful. We constantly have choices — either complain or be grateful, only we can make this choice.

COMPLAINING AND MISTREATMENT

There is a great episode of *Fawlty Towers* (*Waldorf Salad*, I think) — Two old ladies are served some grizzly old meat; it's so overcooked they can barely eat it. When Basil Fawlty (John Cleese) asks if they are enjoying their meal they fake a smile and say "Oh yes, lovely." However, as soon as he turns his back, they screw up their face and spit out the meat. They then start complaining to each other about how bad it is. It is said this is a typical English and Canadian trait — we don't stand up to bad service. We don't say anything outwardly, but we bitterly complain inwardly. This reluctance to complain outwardly has not helped; it just means we complain silently and nurse our grievance. If we have a legitimate grievance it is good to politely and calmly express it. It gives the other person a chance to rectify their bad service and it means we are less likely to nurse a grievance. We need to try to avoid the perpetual inner complaining.

COMPLAINING ABOUT THINGS WE CANNOT CONTROL

There are many things in life which are unjust, unfair and unpleasant. We tend to be drawn to the negative things we see around us and instinctively we start to complain about everything that is wrong. Nevertheless, complaints do not make an iota of difference. They do not change the problem and we just become depressed at the problems in life. There is a big difference between complaining and doing something about it. The old maxim "actions speak louder than words" is oft repeated, but there is much wisdom in that saying. Complaining is essentially a negative act with no positive energy to change things.

COMPLAINTS ARE OFTEN MISINFORMED

Often we complain, but we may complain under false premises. We love to complain about higher taxes, but if we didn't have higher spending on public services like education and health care, we would be complaining about that. It's easy to complain, it's more difficult to do something about it. As another example, we may complain about a difficult person. However, that person could be forcing us to face up to our own weaknesses. Often when we dislike something about another person, their fault exists in our own nature. Rather than complaining we have to learn to deal with difficult people; it may be an opportunity in disguise.

COMPLAINTS DON'T SOLVE ANYTHING

If we tell the waiter the tea is cold, he can heat it up, but most of our complaints do nothing to solve anything. We complain about the amount of litter on the street, but do we ever pick up any litter? We can complain until we are blue in the face about the state of the economy and the government, but this will do nothing to make our life better. If we spent the same energy from complaints into something positive, we would have a chance to make a significant improvement to our life and people around us.

Complaining is essentially a negative, non-constructive activity. It forces us to focus on the negativity, it also often embodies a feeling of powerlessness.

HELP YOURSELF BY SERVING OTHERS

A traditional Indian story tells of a spiritual Master visiting a village. He spoke to the assembled crowds on living a spiritual life. Many were moved by his words on love and forgiveness. However, at the end of the meeting a young child came up to the Master and tearfully asked him if he would come to visit his house and touch the heart of his father. The young child told how his father was making life miserable for the father's wife and children through his uncontrollable drinking. When his father wasn't drinking he was a very kind and loving father, but when he was drunk he made life unbearable for all around. The Master took the child by the hand and visited the pitiful home. He spoke kindly to his mother and her children and then he saw the father lying wretchedly upon a bed of straw. He took the man by his hand and with great kindness said, "Your neighbours on the other side of the town are in sore distress. Their house has been gutted by fire. Will you come and aid me in rebuilding their shattered lives?"

The father shrugged off his headache and feeling of worthlessness and nervously followed the Master to the other side of town. There they found a family facing great hardship due to their loss. Without saying a word, the Master and father began re-building the house. Soon, the drunkard threw himself into the project forgetting his own addictions. After a while the Master thanked the alcoholic for his efforts, but now he had to leave to travel to another town — could he leave him in charge? The father readily agreed and over the next weeks organised the complete rebuilding of the house. In the process, the father gave up drinking completely. Nobody had even mentioned drink, but he had gained a renewed sense of purpose and responsibility. He remained grateful for the opportunity to serve others and overcome his addiction.

COMMENTARY

By lecturing people do we ever change their nature? It is easy to judge others, but how can we encourage people to overcome their weaknesses? It would be tempting to scold an alcoholic for neglecting his family, but here the Master tried a different approach. He sought to rebuild his sense of self-worth and sense of responsibility. Often addictions are symptoms of inner insecurities and we need to deal with these rather than their outer manifestations.

By gaining a sense of service to others we can most easily overcome our personal problems.

It also reminds me of the story of Sri Ramakrishna and his disciple Girish Chandra Ghose. Sri Ramakrishna was a very strict Spiritual Master who expected the highest standards, but in the case of Girish Chandra Ghose, he never said anything when Girish turned up with a wine bottle in his hand. Sri Ramakrishna knew in this particular case, he need not say anything. Over time, by appealing to the good heart of Girish Chandra Ghose, he would eventually make the necessary change in habits himself. This Girish did, becoming a devotee of the highest order.

ENLIGHTENMENT

One of the big downfalls that often happens on the path of self-improvement is a bloated sense of pride. Certainly, it helps to look back and gain confidence from what we have achieved so far. However sometimes, after a nice experience or a good spell in life, we can even feel that we have somehow figured everything out on life's journey, and this kind of complacent feeling can easily lead to our downfall.

WHERE THERE'S AN UP, THERE'S A DOWN

One of the reasons it is important not to be over-elated about any progress you make is that this idea can be very easily shattered by outer circumstances. One common thing that happens is when someone goes to visit some old friends or relatives, they find themselves repeating the same negative cycles of behaviour that used to happen before they embarked on their self-improvement journey, despite all the progress they thought they made! A friend told me something humorous she read recently from one of Eckhart Tolle's books: "If you think you're enlightened, then go and live with your parents for a week."

If you attach too much importance to the good times, you'll attach too much importance to the bad times too, and believe that all your efforts so far were for nought. When it comes to evaluating our inner progress, our human mind is a notoriously bad judge. The best thing is just to keep an even keel throughout both good and bad times.

INNER GROWTH AND HUMILITY GO TOGETHER

Real inner growth always goes hand in hand with an increased sense of humility and selflessness. The focus of everything slowly changes from a selfish one to one more geared towards making the world a better place. Conversely, an exaggerated sense of pride about one's achievements is a bad sign.

ALWAYS HAVE THE ATTITUDE OF A BEGINNER

No matter how far advanced you are along the road of self-discovery, it always pays to have the attitude of a beginner. Every day is a new day, every morning ripe with new possibilities for self-discovery and self-expansion. My own teacher, Sri Chinmoy, meditated for almost seventy years and reached very high levels of meditation, yet he always described himself as "the eternal beginner". No matter what he achieved, every achievement was merely a launch-pad for the next step.

"When we start our journey, the first step forward is our goal. As soon as we reach this goal, we achieve perfection. But today's goal, today's perfection, is tomorrow's starting point; and tomorrow's goal becomes the starting point for the day after tomorrow. Continuous progress is perfection." — Sri Chinmoy

Having the attitude of a beginner allows you to live in the moment, and get joy from the adventure of self-discovery, instead of anticipating an end result.

FORGIVENESS

The capacity for forgiveness is certainly one of the noblest traits we possess as human beings. Despite it commonly being lauded as such throughout the ages, there is however comparatively little examination of the effect an attitude of forgiveness can have on your daily life, both inner and outer.

FORGIVENESS IS PRACTICAL

Forgiveness is often framed as a moral quality, whereas it is first and foremost a practical one. When we are unable to forgive someone who has wronged us, that person retains a kind of power into us, forcing his or her way into our thoughts. "If we spend our time cherishing negative thoughts about someone — jealousy, doubt or anger — then we are making that person our Guru", Sri Chinmoy aptly notes. It is only through forgiveness that we can stop the effects of that action from staying with us long after the original hurt was caused.

Forgiveness allows us to stop dwelling on the person who did the wrong and to get on with our lives. Forgiveness is often not easy — and this article is certainly not intended to slight those who have had serious wrongs done to them and find themselves unable to forgive the wrongdoer. It is, however interesting to read the stories of those who have made that difficult journey to forgiveness. Many of them describe facing a stark choice, either they could be consumed by anger and rage, or try to go beyond it and rebuild their lives.

For most of us, our forgiveness issues will centre on less serious events — someone said something mean about us, or betrayed our trust in some way. In these cases, it helps to remember the times when you have also made the same mistakes. This helps us to feel and understand why they might have done what they did. You might still make a practical decision not to trust them again, but at least that decision can be taken in equanimity and devoid of anger and negativity.

FORGIVING OURSELVES

Often we are our own worst critic, berating ourselves for every little mistake we make in the journey of life. This is often because we compare ourselves to some unreasonable standard of perfection instead of accepting who we are. Forgiving ourselves is part of accepting ourselves and knowing ourselves, and treating our failures as stepping-stones that ultimately lead to our success and growth.

Interestingly enough, the more we can forgive ourselves for our own failing, the more likely we are to accept others for what they are also. Similarly, when you see someone always in the habit of criticising others, you can be sure that they are just as hard on themselves too!

INNER FORGIVENESS

The concept of forgiveness can be very usefully deployed in your inner life, in your practice of prayer or meditation. In meditation, we connect ourselves to a deeper and vaster sense of reality, a reality which does not judge and separate. In this reality only one thing is important, and that is our progress towards becoming a better, kinder and more loving human being.

One good thing to add to your meditation practice (especially at the end of the day) is to invoke inner forgiveness. This does not mean telling yourself what a bad person you are. Instead, it means aspiring to grow beyond the vicious circle of habit that causes us to do things and then regret them later. The more I meditate, the more I see that real outer changes only happen in my life when they are prefaced by a firm inner commitment. This practice cultivates that commitment to rise above repeating the same mistakes. A time will come when, through this aspiration, we finally gain the inner illumination and wisdom to detach our self from whatever it is that causes us to make mistakes, and we gain a profound sense of satisfaction that we are indeed progressing in life's journey.

PART V

MEDITATION

LEARNING MEDITATION

In many of my articles on self-improvement, I often suggest meditation can be an invaluable aid to alleviating many of our daily problems. I don't look upon meditation just as a problem solver; I meditate because I enjoy the consciousness of meditation. If, however, we can gain real peace of mind through meditation, there is no problem that cannot be helped in some way. These are a few preliminary steps for learning how to meditate.

LOCATION

Firstly, find a suitable quiet place for meditation. If it is very hard to find somewhere quiet, use some meditative music to drown out background sounds. If possible, keep a corner of your room reserved just for meditation; this will help build up a meditative vibration in that particular space.

THE BASICS

- It is important to meditate with a straight back. (If you try meditating whilst lying down, you are more likely to fall asleep than entering into a high state of meditation.)
- Don't meditate after eating a heavy meal — you will feel lethargic and sleepy.
- If possible, shower and wear clean clothes before meditating.

- ○ Try to switch off. If you try to meditate straight after work, you may be still thinking about the day. Try reading some books on meditation, written by genuine spiritual Masters and their devotees, to help make the transition from work to meditation.
- ○ If you have difficulty creating time, see: Finding Time for Relaxation / Meditation

RELAXATION

To meditate, it is important to relax and switch off. Tell yourself that for the next 10–15 minutes, you don't have to think about the past or future, just concentrate on the present moment and your meditation. Let go of any tension in your body and try to be fully aware of the present moment. This stage of relaxation is a preliminary stage to meditation, but it is worth emphasising that meditation is more than just relaxation.

BREATHING

The most helpful aid to meditation is proper breathing. Our breathing has a big impact on our mind; if we can quieten our breathing it will help slow down our mind. Focusing on our breathing and nothing else will have a beneficial effect on our meditation. The beauty of meditation is its simplicity. Just be fully conscious of your breathing and feel you are breathing in peace. If you can do this without getting distracted you will be able to meditate most effectively.

LEARNING MEDITATION

THE CALM MIND

> *When you meditate, what you actually do is to enter into*
> *a calm or still, silent mind. We have to be fully aware of*
> *the arrival and attack of thoughts. That is to say, we shall*
> *not allow any thought, divine or undivine, good or bad, to*
> *enter into our mind. Our mind should be absolutely silent.*
> *Then we have to go deep within; there we have to observe*
> *our real existence. .*[21]

With these preliminary stages you can now concentrate on cultivating a calm and quiet mind. This is the essence of meditation and whatever form of meditation you pursue, there will be this common goal of quietening the mind. It is only when we can have a mind free of thoughts that we will be able to experience real meditation. What happens is that when we can quieten the mind we can expand our consciousness and bring the soul to the fore. We feel an expansion of our consciousness, which gives us a good feeling towards the world — this is real meditation.

WHAT IS GOOD MEDITATION?

We can know we are meditating well when we have a good view towards the world. If, however, we feel tension and disturbance then our meditation is not working well. We should have a feeling of simplicity and humility; if we feel proud of ourselves this is not a good sign. Meditation aims to reduce the ego, not expand it.

---

[21] Sri Chinmoy, Earth's Cry Meets Heaven's Smile, Part 1, New York: Agni Press, 1974

BUT MEDITATION IS DIFFICULT

Many newcomers to meditation find it difficult to quieten the mind. This is because the mind is so used to thinking that when we try to stop this, it is quite a shock to the system. If we really want to do something we persevere and practice and meditation is no different; the more we put into meditation the more we will get from it.

WHAT I HAVE LEARNT FROM MEDITATION

I have been practising meditation for 9 years. Since I started, I never recall missing a day. Meditation has become something automatic and instinctive; whatever is happening externally, meditation is a constant undercurrent in my life. During the past 9 years, these are some of the things I have learnt from meditating.

IT IS EASY TO MEDITATE BADLY

It is easy to sit down in meditation and spend 30 minutes with pleasant thoughts going through your mind, but this is not really meditation. Unless there is a conscious and deliberate effort to silence the mind, your meditation is of little benefit. Nobody is going to reward you just for sitting in a chair for a long time. What counts is our ability to silence the mind; this is the essence of meditation, no matter what path we follow.

MEDITATION IS PART PERSONAL EFFORT—PART GRACE

In the beginning we feel meditation is all personal effort, but when we meditate well, we paradoxically feel that we are not making any effort at all. It feels like there is something that is meditating on our behalf. This experience occurs because the soul comes to the fore. Good meditation doesn't involve our mind but our inner being or soul. This is why there is a strange feeling of not actually doing anything.

GOOD MEDITATION ALWAYS WANTS TO SHARE

One of the most surprising features of meditation is that when you meditate well, there is an unmistakable desire to inwardly share this consciousness with others. There is an instinctive feeling that the peace you experience also belongs to others. It is not possible to separate the meditative consciousness and keep it for yourself. Meditation expands our sense of awareness; it gives an unexpected sense of connection with other people. This is not a mere intellectual idea of oneness; but something that can only ever be felt and experienced.

GRATITUDE

If you have a powerful meditation there is a strong sense of gratitude; this is much more than our usual polite way of saying "Thank you". It is a spontaneous feeling that our meditation is a gift which we can only feel gratitude for.

THE EGO WANTS TO SPOIL MEDITATION

It is quite common that good meditation becomes spoilt by the intervention of the ego. Our meditation may go very well, but then the ego starts to spoil it by creating a sense of spiritual pride. When we feel pride in our meditation, we know it has taken a wrong turn. To meditate well, we have to give up all idea and concept of displaying anything to other people. When we meditate well there is no desire for anyone to outwardly know. Meditation is something sacred that can only be shared inwardly. In the best meditation there is no sense of self; perhaps momentarily we forget about our sense of "i-ness". We feel that the meditation is impersonal, and just about consciousness.

THE WORLD MAKES SENSE

It seems justice has never been born in the outer world, and perhaps never will. But in meditation, there is a feeling that somehow everything makes sense and will work out. I cannot explain this or even attempt to justify it with words; but, that is definitely an experience of meditation.

THERE IS NOTHING TO LEARN

I remember a couple of meditations where the only feeling was that I was merely remembering something I always had. The meditation did not give me anything new, it was merely the recollection of something from a distant past. At the same time, there was a feeling, "Why had this innocence and sense of being ever been lost?"

INSPIRATION

There are many techniques for meditation; but the real secret of meditation is the inner cry, the aspiration to transcend the mental world. This inspiration can come in many forms, but it is far more powerful than any technique.

MEDITATION IN EVERYDAY LIFE

The mind wants to criticise and feel a sense of separativity. Meditation encourages us to live in the heart and forget mistakes and criticism. I often feel a split personality in life. The mind is prone to depression and negativity; the heart just experiences, without negativity. Life is a constant choice between the two. Meditation encourages us to forget the pedantic criticisms of the mind and to live in the heart. Once we have experienced real inner peace, we become more sensitive to cherishing the opposites, anger and frustration.

MUSIC AND MEDITATION

The right kind of meditative music can definitely inspire our meditation. I am fortunate to have access to many excellent recordings of meditation music. The highest meditation is in absolute silence, but meditating to appropriate music can definitely inspire us.

PSYCHIC CENTRES

In many spiritual books you will read about the seven main *chakras* or energy centres. Through meditation these centres can be opened, at least partially; they can be felt as a real physical sensation. My meditation teacher, Sri Chinmoy, advises meditating on the spiritual heart or *anahata chakra*; this is in the centre of the chest, near the physical heart. In meditation we can feel the energy of the spiritual heart, an uplifting sensation of the energy spinning and revolving. It is an excellent thing to focus on during meditation.

MEDITATION AND SLEEP

Meditating when you are sleepy doesn't work. For meditation you have to be awake and alert. Meditation is a heightening of awareness; it is completely opposite to the relaxation of being unconscious.

MEDITATION HAS NO FIXED GOAL

After meditating for 10 years, I feel I have barely made it to the starting line. There have been good experiences, there have been times when meditation has proved difficult. Yet, there is also a feeling that I have only experienced a glimpse of the real consciousness of meditation. Reading the writings of saints and spiritual masters gives an insight into the nature of pure consciousness and encourages us to strive for more.

THERE IS AN UNDERLYING UNITY IN RELIGIOUS / SPIRITUAL EXPERIENCES

If we examine the scriptures and religions of the world with our mind, we see many differences and even conflict. In contrast, meditation teaches us to place less emphasis on outer ritual and more on the inner experience. Therefore the meditation of a Christian saint can offer the same consciousness as the meditation of a Sufi or Buddhist. The way we approach the goal doesn't matter, as ultimately we are aiming for the same goal, the same consciousness. It is impossible to describe meditation, because the experience far transcends the mind; no words can ever do it justice, although through poetry and other writings we can get a glimpse, an inkling of what lies within.

THE ABSOLUTE

No mind, no form, I only exist;
Now ceased all will and thought;
The final end of Nature's dance,
I am it whom I have sought

A realm of Bliss bare, ultimate;
Beyond both knower and known;
A rest immense I enjoy at last;
I face the One alone.

I have crossed the secret ways of life,
I have become the Goal.
The Truth immutable is revealed;
I am the way, the God-Soul.

My spirit aware of all the heights,
I am mute in the core of the Sun.
I barter nothing with time and deeds;
My cosmic play is done.[22]

---

[22] Sri Chinmoy, My Flute, The Absolute, New York: Agni Press, 1972

YOUR OWN THOUGHTS

Quite often we find ourselves with many negative thoughts going through our mind. These trains of thoughts can become very powerful as we endlessly repeat them in our mind. The problem is that the more we focus on the thoughts, the more powerful they become. Therefore, it can become very difficult to stop these endless cycles of thoughts. However, it is definitely possible and these are a few tips to control our thoughts.

MAKE A CONSCIOUS DECISION TO STOP THE THOUGHTS

Sometimes we attach ourselves to certain ideas and problems, and we subconsciously get a kind of pleasure from going through a certain problem / issue. If we subconsciously keep inviting the thoughts, we will never be able to stop them. Therefore, the first stage is to make a clear and conscious decision to stop the repetition of the thoughts. Be aware of their negative impact and don't allow them to come any more. This conscious step is an indispensable stage in controlling our thoughts.

LOOK UPON THOUGHTS AS BEING OUTSIDE OF YOURSELF

When we first try to stop the thoughts, it seems very difficult because they feel such a strong part of our mind. Therefore, the second stage is to feel that the thoughts are separate to our self. When a thought appears in your mind, look upon the thought as coming from outside yourself. This is a powerful way to reduce the impact of thoughts on our mind. Once we realise our thoughts are separate to ourselves we can stop them.

WHO IS IT WHO LISTENS TO THOUGHTS?

This is a technique to try and discover the origination of your thoughts. Whenever a thought appears, just ask yourself, who is it who is thinking this? What we do is to try and discover the source of thoughts. Through asking this question we realise that there is an "I" which can decide to accept or reject thoughts. By asking this question we will be able to stop the thoughts as soon as they enter. You are not a victim of your own thoughts, it is you who either rejects or gives life to thoughts.

CATCH THOUGHTS AS SOON AS THEY APPEAR

This exercise requires a determined effort on our part. We need to be vigilant and watch every thought that enters our mind. As soon as we see a negative thought enter, we must immediately discard it and refuse to follow it. The more we follow thoughts, the more difficult it becomes to stop them later. Therefore, it is best to catch them as soon as possible.

CONCENTRATE ON SOMETHING ELSE

If a train of thoughts have gained a stranglehold over our mind, the best solution is often to just try and do something completely different. Don't just sit around, go and do something which gives you no opportunity to ruminate over your thoughts. By doing this, we ignore the thoughts completely and they lose there hold over us.

MEDITATION

Meditation is the best way to learn how to control our thoughts. Meditation involves the art of concentration and quietening the mind. In meditation we not only try to control our thoughts but we also can bring to the fore our inner qualities of peace and oneness. If we can invoke the calming power of our own heart, then we use this alternative force to take the place of the negative mind.

We should meditate every day so that we can bring to the fore as much as peace as possible into our mind. If we meditate only when we are overrun with thoughts we will find meditation very difficult, whereas if we gain peace of mind through our daily meditation then we develop our inner capacities to control our thoughts.

A CONCENTRATION EXERCISE

Concentration is the secret key to a whole world of possibilities, enabling you to keep out distractions and focus on attaining your life goals. In addition, it is an absolute prerequisite if you want to learn the art of meditation. Here is one very easy-to-learn concentration exercise which was taught to me by my meditation teacher Sri Chinmoy. See: *Meditation: Man Perfection in God Satisfaction* (1989) by Sri Chinmoy.

It can reap tremendous rewards in terms of clarity, productivity and efficiency in your life, and it can be done with just a few minutes practise every day. People commonly view concentration as purely a mental exercise; but here we are also going use our heart centre, that space in our chest we point to when we say "me"—helping to take some of the burden away from our tension-filled minds.

REQUIREMENTS

An object of concentration — it is best to use a candle or flower, but you can even use a dot on the wall.

METHOD

In this exercise, we will use the candle, although you can adapt the exercise to whatever object you are using. Sit with your back straight, and place the burning candle at eye level.

First bring your awareness to your breath. Gradually your breath becomes slower and more relaxed.

Try to imagine a thread placed in front of our nose ; you are breathing so quietly it will not move to and fro. Now look at the object.

Gradually bring your attention to a tiny part of the candle flame, for example, the very tip of the flame. When you breathe in, feel that your breath, like a golden thread, is coming from that point on the candle and entering into your heart.

When you breath out, feel that your breath, feel that the light is leaving the heart, passing through a point in your forehead between the eyebrows and a little above (in Eastern philosophy this is a powerful concentration point) and then entering into the object of concentration.

Try to feel that nothing else exists except you and the object you are focusing on.

When you do this exercise, thoughts will invariably get in the way. When this happens, don't be annoyed or upset, just bring your attention back to the exercise. Rome wasn't built in a day, and similarly it will take time to rein in your mind.

*

(*If you have the time*) You can go one step further, and use your power of concentration to identify with the object's existence.

Try to feel on the in-breath that the existence of the flame, and the qualities it embodies such as radiance, serenity and aspiration, are entering into you and becoming part of your own existence.

On the out-breath, feel that your existence is expanding and spreading out from the centre of the chest and entering into the candle.

In this way, you concentrate on the object to such an extent that you feel no separation between you and the object; your existence has expanded to include the candle. In this way you can identify our self with the entire world.

THE INNER VOICE

There are few greater challenges than working out what is the right thing to do. Sometimes it can appear quite difficult working out what to choose. These are some suggestions for following our inner conscience and creating the life which will give us most satisfaction.

BE STILL

To listen to the inner voice, we have to be able to still the mind and quieten our conflicting thoughts. We need to have a faith that something within us has the wisdom to know the right thing. To listen to our inner voice, we can try this technique: Repeat the question you need answered very carefully in silence and then try to maintain an inner silence for at least 5 minutes; we should not allow any thought to enter, but keep our mind absolutely quiet. At the end of our silent meditation we should have a clearer idea about what to do.

DOES IT GIVE YOU PEACE OR ANXIETY?

If we feel inwardly awkward about a certain course of action, this is a sign that we are doing the wrong thing. When we are doing the right thing, it will be accompanied by a sense of inner peace. Even if others may not appreciate our action, as long as we are acting with the right motives and intentions, we will have a clear conscience and a sense of peace with our decision.

ASK YOURSELF THE QUESTION

Sometimes we never even stop to think about the right thing to do, but rush headlong into choosing without even thinking. We need to take the time to stop and consider; any worthwhile decision can be given at least a few minutes' thought and reflection.

DON'T ACT UNDER THE WRONG IMPULSE

Sometimes we instinctively know the right thing to do, but we make a decision that is clouded by a negative emotion such as anger. When we are overwhelmed with anger, our judgement is blurred and we are prone to acting in a way that exacerbates the situation. Often we regret responding in anger because it creates conflict. If something is the right thing to do we will want to do it even after calmly evaluating the situation.

DOES IT FIT THE ETERNAL VALUES?

There are certain precepts and ancient teachings which have always resonated with humanity. These have been expressed in different forms and people will have faith in particular teachings. For complicated decisions we can evaluate our decision against these sayings of wisdom. For example, how does our decision affect other people? The golden rule is "Do unto others, as you would have done to you." If our decisions fit in with this precept then that is a very good sign.

MOTIVE

It is easy for our mind to justify our wrong actions; we need to be very careful of this. If our mind is being very defensive and is working on a justification for our actions, we have to be especially vigilant. Only we ourselves can know our inner motive. Here we have to be honest with ourselves; if we try to deceive ourselves that we are being selfless, it will only cause problems and make us foolish. If we are acting to further our social standing or to gain at the expense of others, we have to be very critical of our motives.

DON'T WORRY TOO MUCH

Sometimes sensitive people can worry too much about the right thing to do. Often the most important thing is not the actual decision, but the motive and consciousness behind what we do. Whatever we decide to do, we should try to do it with enthusiasm and kindness. If we act with the right intentions, then we can make even the most insignificant actions meaningful. If we are miserable and mean, then whatever we choose to do we will not be helpful to anyone.

LIVING IN THE HEART

In western society, the mind is generally considered to be the apex of our being, and deep thinkers are celebrated as the defining product of our times. In fact, it was not until I was in my mid-twenties that I came across the notion that the ordinary human mind may not be the be-all and end-all of human existence. What could possibly lie beyond the mind, I wondered? Well, we unconsciously answer that question every day when we gesture towards ourselves during a conversation — we point towards the middle of the chest, the place where we intuitively feel the core of our being. Hence if you are interested in pursuing the possibilities of self-discovery, then learning to live in the heart is a very good place to start.

SO WHAT DIFFERENTIATES THE HEART FROM THE MIND?

Empathy. The heart is the place where we feel a sense of connectedness and goodwill with other people and the world — the phrase "my heart goes out to him" says it all, I think. This is in stark contrast to the mind, which quite often resorts to stereotyping and seeing the bad qualities in others.

Oneness. The mind works by gathering information, then classifying and categorising — a process of dividing which ultimately separates you from the object you are looking at. The heart, on the other hand, expands to identify itself with an object or situation, such that you actually feel connected with the thing you are focusing on.

Spontaneity. The mind can become very jaded with seeing the same things and constantly requires new excitement to keep it happy; newness and freshness are an intrinsic part of the heart's nature. For the heart, everything happens in the now — no mulling over the past, no worrying about what might happen. We can see this most clearly with children, running around inventing new games and discarding them in favour of new ones at the spur of the moment.

Purpose. Often we have difficulty finding a purpose to fulfil here on earth, the thing that will make us most happy. The mind is very often no help here, vacillating between one option and another, heavily influenced by the unrealistic expectations of other people or society. Yet when we quieten the mind, we can feel an inner inspiration coming from the depths of our existence. When we get such an inspiration, it is often accompanied by a tremendous sense of inner joy and relief that replaces our mental indecision. There is also a sense of certainty that does not depend on the result of the action; we inwardly know it is the right thing to do, regardless of whether it meets with success or failure.

SO HOW DOES ONE EXPLORE THE REALM OF THE HEART?

Here are a few exercises to practice for a few minutes every day.

1. Use the breath. It is in the silence of the mind that you can then bring your attention to the heart. I found this simple breathing exercise to be quite effective: as you breathe in, follow the river of breath as it enters through the nose into the core of your being. Similarly, on the out breath, feel the

river of breath leaving your heart centre and leaving through your mouth into the universe.

2. No mind. Let the power of imagination point you towards the heart centre. Feel and imagine that you have no mind, all you have is the heart; you can repeat to yourself "I have no mind; all I have is the heart". After a few minutes you can go even further and say, "I am the heart", firmly identifying yourself with this reality in the core of your being.

3. Mantras. In Eastern traditions this is considered one of the most effective ways to get into the heart. You can use ancient Sanskrit terms like *Aum* or *Shanti* (meaning peace) or instead repeat some quality of the heart that you particularly like, such as "Love" or "Joy".

   If you place your hands on your chest whilst saying it; the physical sensation of the voice helps to bring your attention to the heart centre. As you repeat, feel that it is actually your heart centre saying the mantra in and through you.

4. Music. Different kinds of music tend to affect different parts of our being, like our mind or our emotions. Likewise, music created by people who live in the heart tends to also elevate our awareness and bring us closer to the heart.

   Just as the tide gets under a boat and lifts it up, so music can elevate you to places of peace and beauty inside yourself. When listening, resist all temptation to analyse the music and, in the words of Sri Chinmoy, *"Let the music-bird fly inside your heart-sky"*.

PART VI

COMMUNICATION

BETTER COMMUNICATION

SMILING HELPS ANY CONVERSATION

Sometimes silence is a much underrated quality but, everything has its time and place. Good communication is essential for dealing with others. These are some tips for better communication.

AVOID UNNECESSARY WORDS

We pepper our speech with unnecessary words. "You know some people say...." I mean...." Sometimes less is more, these extra words can also sound condescending. Speak plainly.

SPEAK CLEARLY

There is nothing more frustrating than a conversation which is half heard. Always try to speak clearly. If someone asks you to repeat yourself once, make a special effort, because often people will not ask more than once out of a sense of embarrassment.

BE WARY OF SPEAKING HARSHLY

If you are really disappointed with someone, you can express your disappointment/frustration without anger or bitterness. The other person will be much more receptive to your message delivered with sweetness — or at least the absence of anger and disgust. Sometimes it is more beneficial to take the compassionate approach rather than the justice approach. People may deserve a harsh lesson, but would it actually help?

AVOIDING UNNECESSARY COMMUNICATION

It is good to communicate well, but you can have too much of a good thing. Don't bombard friends with unnecessary text messages. Be confident in your friendship rather than looking for constant reassurance.

METHOD OF COMMUNICATION

In a digital age, we tend to gravitate towards the most convenient communication, but this can be the least personal and least effective. An electronic message has much greater scope for misinterpretation and misunderstanding than speaking to someone in person. The next time you say something satirical or sarcastic to a friend, try to imagine sending that message in an email. You can guarantee that without the benefit of facial expression and human contact the message would be misinterpreted.

DIFFICULT COMMUNICATION

There are many times when we want to say something, but put it off because of nervousness, a desire to avoid difficult situations, or a feeling of guilt for having to tell someone off. However, putting off communication often just makes it worse. What tends to happen is that when we put off speaking to someone, our mind just magnifies the problems, turning a small issue into a big problem. Our mind speculates on many adverse reactions which are false. If we find ourselves in this situation, the best thing is to speak sooner rather than later.

SUGGESTIONS FOR DIFFICULT COMMUNICATION

Let go of negative expectations — they will probably be wrong anyway. Just speak with kind intentions. If you have the other person's best interests at heart, then whatever you have to say will be easier to say. Also, if you have good will towards the other person, then you can easily let go of all guilt that may be blocking you from speaking to that person. Remember the positive things that will occur from bringing up difficult situations. The other person may appreciate your intervention at some time — even if not now.

Let go of a feeling of pride. Don't feel the conversation is about having to defend yourself or prove yourself and put the other person down. This kind of attitude is guaranteed to create an awkward situation. Be self-giving and give no importance to silly human pride.

IT'S NOT WHAT YOU SAY, BUT HOW YOU SAY IT

Suppose you have to tell someone they have been doing something wrong. There are two approaches. The first is to exaggerate the extent of their mistake and try to make them feel guilty for doing such a silly thing. The other approach is to start off by saying it is the kind of mistake you could have made yourself. Even if you say a white lie and say you once did the same thing, who will be hurt? If you think about both approaches, you will know exactly how you would want to be treated should someone tell about your misdemeanours.

SIMPLICITY

In modern life there are seemingly endless series of options and avenues. At each turn, life seems to present numerous complications. It becomes hard to resist the allure of doing more things and trying to solve a myriad of problems. However, we are often consciously or unconsciously yearning for a more simple approach to life. If we can make an effort to bring more simplicity into our lives, we will find that many benefits arise.

PEACE OF MIND

Simplicity doesn't necessarily involve living in a spartan hut. Real simplicity begins in the mind. If we have numerous anxieties and problems it is not possible to have peace of mind. Simplicity means we learn to clear the mind and not allow ourselves to be bombarded by an endless stream of needless thoughts.

LIVING IN THE PRESENT

Complication in life often arises because we are worrying and planning about the future. We can become so concerned about what may happen tomorrow or next year that we forget to enjoy the present moment. To have one's focus on the here and now, is to encompass life as it is supposed to be.

LESS PLANNING AND THINKING

When we complicate life through our endless planning, we bring tomorrow's problems into today. Yet it is always worth remembering that our worries and fears about the future often prove to be groundless.

AVOIDING JUDGEMENT

It is part of human nature to criticise and judge other people. It is very easy to make a long list of complaints and suggestions about other people. But does it help us when we highlight the faults of others? We should feel that we are not responsible for other people's thoughts and behaviour. If we feel it is our bounden duty to change others, there can be no simplicity and peace in our life. Rather than try to change others, let us just try to focus on changing ourselves. Our own weaknesses are probably more than enough to deal with.

FOCUS AND ACHIEVEMENT

Simplicity enables more to be achieved. Simplicity means that we are focused on one thing at a time. Simplicity means we can put all our concentration on just one thing. If we perform an action with no distractions then we can fulfil it quicker and more successfully. Often, when we simplify our life, we find we can actually achieve more than when we juggled several things at once.

> *The simpler we can become, the sooner we shall reach our destination. A life of simplicity is a life of constant progress. It is in simplicity that we can make the fastest progress, progress which is everlasting.* .[23]

---

[23] Sri Chinmoy, Life-Tree-Leaves, New York: Agni Press, 1974

SIMPLICITY AND BEAUTY

Simplicity is often synonymous with beauty. For example, Zen gardens are uncluttered and simple, yet in that simplicity there is a beauty which appeals to our soul. It is the same with Mother Nature; the essence of nature is its unspoilt beauty. Has man ever been able to improve on the beauty and simplicity of nature?

HAPPINESS

Be happy with what we have. As George Bernard Shaw aptly stated,

> *There are two tragedies in life. One is not to get your heart's desire; the other is to get it.* .[24]

The nature of desire is that the more we get the more we want. When we get a new car, after a while we are not satisfied and want to get something better. However, real happiness comes when we are content with what we have and are free of desire.

---

[24] George Bernard Shaw, Man and Superman" act 4, London, Penguin Classics: 2001

CLEARING OUT YOUR CLUTTER

Is your workplace surrounded by useless stuff and clutter that you find difficult to get rid of? If you have been planning to unclutter your room, these are some tips to make sure you can actually do it.

DO I NEED IT? IS IT BEAUTIFUL?

Do you really need the item? Is the item of intrinsic beauty? Even by just asking these questions we can help to decide whether we really need it. Unfortunately, we often accumulate things without questioning whether we really need them. Go through each item; if you cannot justify its use then get rid of it without any qualms.

START WITH NOTHING AND ADD ONLY WHAT YOU NEED.

Another very effective way to remove unnecessary clutter is to start from scratch. Rather than looking at things to throw away, imagine the room was completely bare, and then only add what you really need. This is a great way to decide whether a thing is of practical importance or just there out of habit.

BEAUTY IN SIMPLICITY

To get rid of clutter you should try and keep in your mind a vision of a better alternative. If you have something to aspire for, it will become much easier to throw things away. If you really value the beauty of simplicity then it will be effortless to make this a reality. Look at catalogues of dream houses, in these "show piece settings" you won't see piles of old newspapers, unwashed coffee cups and piles of dirty laundry.

DON'T BE OVERLY SENTIMENTAL

Do you really need to keep your school notes from Grade 5? Unless you are likely to reread elementary geometry in the next 12 months, you can probably chuck out these painful memories of old school days. This doesn't mean you have to throw everything away. Do keep things of great sentimental value, but don't feel guilty about not keeping everything.

CHOOSE TOP TEN ITEMS

If you have difficulty throwing ornamental things away, why not try making a list of just your favourite top 7 or top 3 items? This forces you to be ruthless and only keep the things that you really want.

ORGANISATION

Sometimes it is not just a matter of throwing things away, but being organised. Items which are rarely used, can be put in the most distant storage space like a garage or attic. Add extra shelves and keep things organised.

GIVE TO CHARITY

Giving unwanted items to a charity shop is an excellent way of creating space for yourself and making a useful contribution to charity. Just make sure you don't buy more bric-a-brac when you give your own items away.

SELL

If you want to make money from your accumulated stuff, try selling it to someone who might value it more.

GET YOUR MOTHER TO COME ROUND

Maybe your mother is not the best person, but sometimes an independent third party can give a different perspective and help point out obvious improvements that we have become blind to.

CLEAR UP AS YOU GO

Don't wait for the day when you have "loads of time" — that day may never come. Try to keep on top of your living space all the time. Once it is tidy and spacious, it provides its own incentive to avoid cluttering it up. Don't delay but start right now.

HOW TO AVOID PROCRASTINATION

Procrastination — "To delay and put off doing what could be done now, especially out of habitual carelessness or laziness. Often associated with feelings of guilt."

To some extent we all engage in procrastination, but if we are not careful, procrastination can easily become a habit that we are not even aware of. Yet, when we procrastinate we in a state of limbo; neither enjoying a period of relaxation nor gaining the satisfaction of achieving something.

WHY DO WE PROCRASTINATE?

The first reason we procrastinate is that we aim for perfection, but feel this perfection is not possible for us to achieve. Because we want to attain perfection, we feel we are justified in waiting until we are in a better frame of mind, or circumstances are more favourable. However, when we wait for circumstances to be "just right" we may never start at all. Related to this aim of perfection is the fear of failure or fear of living up to our high expectations. Subconsciously we do not want to start, because we feel we will be embarrassed or let down by our achievements. This fear of failure can be exacerbated by concerns over what others may think. Therefore, rather than risk disappointment, we put off doing the task at all.

Another reason for procrastination is that we prefer to do things that are easier and more enjoyable. Procrastination is often most serious when we are completing our academic studies; there are many more enjoyable things to do than write essays.

Procrastination is made even easier when we are working on the internet. Technology like the internet gives us many options to spend time without much effort. Therefore, we can easily spend time surfing the internet and checking emails; these tasks are much less effort than doing something productive.

HOW TO OVERCOME PROCRASTINATION

The first thing is to be aware of is how much we procrastinate. Sometimes, we can make ourselves feel that we are doing something productive, but if we are honest with ourselves, playing solitaire is not going to help us write that best selling novel. When we are aware of how much we procrastinate, we should set clear priorities of what we wish to do first. It is not procrastination if we seek to do something which is more important. If we have clear targets and work on them before anything else, then we can enjoy our relaxation, without the guilt which comes with procrastination.

A second method to overcoming procrastination is to be single minded, and not allow ourselves to get distracted by less important things. If we do just one thing at a time, we can achieve it more quickly and with less hesitation.

Perhaps the most helpful suggestion for overcoming procrastination is to force ourselves to make a start; even if our first attempts are less than perfect.

Once we can actually get started we may find that we gain in confidence. As soon as we start and focus on just our highest priority, we often find it is less difficult than we imagined. Also, we should always bear in mind that procrastination will never help us in any way.

CREATING BETTER HABITS

We are creatures of habit, but unfortunately the habits we pick up often limit our happiness and sense of fulfilment. The worst habit we can have is the inability to make any changes, but continue with a perpetual negative attitude. If we can recognise our own bad habits we can create the necessary steps to making meaningful changes in our life. The following are some of our most common bad habits in modern life.

CONSTANTLY BUSY

Is your life constantly hectic with a never-ending strain on your time and nerves? Do you have time to enjoy the finer things of life? Sometimes, even the most financially successful people find it difficult to create leisure time where they can relax and be at peace. It is always possible to create activity and things to do, but many of these activities are invariably non-essential. Modern technology is supposed to help make life easier, not make us constantly busy. Learn how to let go of things like email addiction — create time for yourself and your own relaxation.

GETTING UP LATE

The best part of the day is often the morning. Yet, the mind and body can be uncooperative, causing us to sleep in for longer than necessary. It is a shame to waste so many hours. Create good sleeping habits that help you to get up early in the morning. Once you have got used to more hours in the morning, you will not want to go back to having more sleep than necessary.

WORRYING ABOUT MONEY

We cannot avoid financial issues, but we can prevent them from dominating our lives. Sometimes money worries occur because we create ever-increasing levels of personal debt. This can be due to unnecessary overspending or poor financial management. Don't feel happiness is dependent on levels of consumption; if we avoid overspending and creating debt we can avoid much mental anguish. At the other end of the scale, even people who are financially successful can still give too much priority to money. There is more to life than just earning money; don't use every moment of your life to think how you can increase your wealth.

LAZY DIET

Our diet doesn't just affect our physical health but also our mental health. Experiment with a fast food diet, and then a diet of healthy, well-cooked food and notice the difference. Also, we become accustomed to the food we eat. If we eat a lot of salty, fatty and sugary foods, this is what the mind tends to crave and so we eat more and more. However, if we can break these habits and eat good foods for a couple of weeks, we will be pleasantly surprised to find that we actually lose our taste for double cheeseburgers and fries; we will get much more pleasure from eating wholesome foods.

The important thing here is the willingness to change, and not just continue with a diet because it is what we have done in the past.

ADDICTION TO COMPUTER GAMES

It is easy to pass several hours playing solitaire on our computer, but after playing even the most advanced computer games, do we gain a feeling of real satisfaction and achievement? It is easy to get in the habit of playing computer games, but may later regret spending so much time. Computer games have an addictive quality we don't always like to admit to. They can give a limited pleasure, but if we allow them to dominate our lives there will always be a feeling of something lacking.

SELF CRITICISM

Self-criticism can be beneficial if we look at our habits in a measured way. The process of self-inquiry is essential for overcoming bad habits and learning to improve. However, self-criticism can become harmful if it becomes an irrational self-hatred. The mind can exaggerate the smallest mistakes and make them appear very harmful; this kind of attitude lowers our self-esteem and creates an unhealthy feeling of guilt. Learn from your mistakes, but avoid beating yourself up at the same time.

DEFENSIVE MECHANISM

How do you respond to any kind of criticism? Often our instinctive approach is to build up a defensive mechanism where we seek to avoid feelings of hurt and injured pride. If we are always defensive and rigid we make life difficult for ourselves. We falsely equate our happiness with proving that we are right. Our pride becomes a barrier to making change and learning from our mistakes. Let go of the desire to always have the last word; don't worry so much about your self-image and pride; happiness does not depend on the constant appreciation of the world....

HOW TO GET UP EARLY IN THE MORNING

To get up early in the morning is a real boon. Most people would appreciate more time; after all, most tasks are more useful than sleeping. However, to get up early in the morning is not always easy, especially if we are used to lying in.

As as a student I got into the habit of sleeping in late, waking up and then going back to snooze for "just" another half an hour. However, that the extra half an hour doesn't give you any more energy; it can even make you feel more lethargic.

If we are determined to get up early we can consider the following tips.

SET THE ALARM AT A REGULAR TIME EACH DAY

The body is a creature of habit, if we develop the routine of getting up at a certain time, then it becomes easier and more natural to wake up at our target time. If we are not used to waking up early, it may be a shock to the system. It is important, however, to persevere and continue getting up at this time — even at the weekends. By getting up at the same time each day it helps to set the body clock. If we are lucky there may come a time when we spontaneously wake up early.

BE CAREFUL WITH THE SNOOZE BUTTON

It is better to set the alarm and get up at that time. If we keep pressing the snooze button it becomes difficult to get up. When we lie in bed hoping to get an extra 10 minutes' rest, we are not actually sleeping. The longer we doze, the more difficult it becomes to get up.

One trick is to put the alarm clock at the far end of the room. This means to turn it off you actually have to get out of bed — don't make it easy to go back to sleep.

BE MOTIVATED TO GET UP

The key to getting up early in the morning is our desire to get up early. If we are really motivated to wake up at a certain time, we will not let the mind create excuses for going back to sleep. It is worth making a list of things we can do early in the morning. Early morning can be productive because the environment of the house is usually quieter. Whatever your personal list maybe, it's probably better than sleeping in. If we really value the benefits of getting up early, we will make it happen.

REINFORCE THE TIME JUST BEFORE SLEEPING

Before you go to bed at night repeat to your mind the intended time of getting up. If you really focus on a particular time, such as 6.00am, it can influence the subconscious mind. When we repeat the target time several times, it becomes a powerful mantra to help us get up at that time.

GO TO BED WHEN TIRED

Just because you want to get up earlier doesn't mean you have to go to sleep earlier. Quite often we sleep more than necessary. It is better to only go to sleep when we feel tired. If we go to bed early when we are not tired, we will just waste time trying to sleep; this will not help getting up in the morning.

STRETCHING

On waking up it is a good idea to get straight out of bed and undertake a few stretches or light exercise. By stretching we help the circulation of blood, it can make us feel less dozy and will discourage us from going straight back to sleep. It has been suggested that taking a cold bath or shower will also be of tremendous benefit in waking up, however the author of this article cannot personally vouch for this method.

TRICK THE MIND

Many people say it is easier to get up in the morning during the summer months. If this is the case, try to make your room an inviting place to wake up. If it is really cold, use an instant heater to turn on as soon as you wake up. Also, when you wake up, turn on several lights — for greater effect try using natural sunlight bulbs. If the room is warm and light, diving back under the covers will be less attractive.

Getting up early in the morning may be difficult at first; however, if we persevere we will really appreciate the extra time it creates. To get up early the most important thing is to value its benefits. If we are really determined to get up early we will fight the lethargy of the body and make sure we actually get up when the alarm clock goes off.

MOTIVATION

Enthusiasm and motivation are key principles for getting anything done. If we are motivated and committed we find ways to get round obstacles. If we lack motivation then we easily find difficulties and excuses to give up. To increase our motivation we really need to be clear what we want to do. These are some tips to increase your motivation.

BE CLEAR WHAT YOU WISH TO ACHIEVE

It is important to know what is important to you. Think carefully about what really matters. If you consciously give something a high priority, then this is half the battle for gaining motivation. We often struggle to gain motivation for an activity or issue because we are not clear in our mind about what we wish to achieve. For example, we may go through life with a vague idea that it would be good to get up earlier in the morning, but only if we really see benefits will we have motivation.

TEJVAN PETTINGER

JUST ACT!

We can only be fully committed to a certain number of things; we need to prioritise what is important. However, whilst it is important to be aware of life's priorities, we don't want to spend too long just thinking. If we sit around planning and thinking, the mind will find innumerable problems and complications which reduce our motivation. The best thing is to get started and throw yourself wholeheartedly into a project. Once you get started and focus on a project, it develops a certain energy which is self reinforcing.

I teach Economics and many of my students say how worried they are about the exams and how they haven't time. In fact, their real problem is just to get started with work and revision. The worst is just sitting around saying how little time we have.

DON'T RELY ON EXTERNAL PRAISE

Often we lack motivation because we feel our efforts are not fully recognised. To be willing to work without praise is a real blessing. The secret is to feel the satisfaction from doing the right thing and giving ourselves the opportunity for our self-improvement. We shouldn't just be motivated for the end result, but for the challenge of getting there. Be kind to yourself and notice the satisfaction you gain from doing the right thing with the right attitude; this will always be worth more than the fleeting praise of others.

SATISFACTION

Lasting motivation will come when we get joy from doing something. The problem is we often feel that worthwhile changes or projects require self-discipline, sacrifice and difficulties. It is this which discourages and de-motivates. We need to change our attitude: rather than thinking of the sacrifice or discipline we need to undergo, focus on the lasting sense of achievement we get.

REMOVE DISTRACTIONS

To increase our motivation to do something useful, we often need to avoid the distractions that pull us away into insignificant things. After sitting in front of the TV for an hour flicking through channels or surfing useless internet sites, it is remarkable how much motivation can disappear!

BE OF SERVICE

If we only think of ourself then it is hard to do difficult things. However, if we really try to emphathise with others then it is much easier to be motivated to make difficult changes.

UNDERSTAND COSTS AND BENEFITS

We have a tendency to stumble from one crisis to the next. If we get stomach pains we reach for the stomach pills rather than looking at our diet. Often we need motivation for activities where benefits are long term and costs are short term. Looking after our health, for example, will give much benefit returns in the long term. We just need to remind ourselves of the costs and benefits.

IRRATIONAL THINKING
AND HOW TO OVERCOME IT

One of the biggest problems we have is the tendency for our mind to think in an irrational or unbalanced way. We see issues and other people through a clouded and fuzzy perspective. This judgement leads us to many problems; not least it makes life more stressful and depressing. These are some of the common perspectives on life which are misleading.

JUMPING TO CONCLUSIONS

Often we jump to conclusions after only a small fraction of evidence. Perhaps someone does not reply to our message at a particular point in time, we then project our own thoughts as to why this is. The mind creates a powerful scenario which we come to believe. Yet, our mental projections are often far from reality. To make things worse, we often jump to conclusions in a negative way. The mind is suspicious of others' intentions and we definitely create problems for ourselves by doubting our friends and relatives.

We have to be very wary of jumping to conclusions; at the very least we should remind ourself that our conclusion is likely to be wrong. It may be unfortunate to be mistreated by others, but it is much worse to have a suspicious mind.

BLACK AND WHITE THINKING

We often come to see the world in black and white terms — either we are a total success or failure. Other people are either friends or enemies. Perhaps one small mistake can make us feel a total failure. For example, we say one wrong thing so then assume we have messed up a relationship with someone. On the other hand a small success can bloat us with pride. Life is never so clear cut; we have to avoid both the depths of despair and heights of vainglory. Rather than seeing ourselves as a total failure, just see mistakes as stepping-stones on the path to self-development.

BLAMING OTHER PEOPLE FOR OUR OWN FAULTS

Often we sit in judgement over other people, but if we were honest we would realise many of their faults we too share. We are not judging out of compassion but out of a sense of self-importance. The worst thing is when we do something wrong but seek to pass the blame onto other people — if only other people had done the right thing, we would be fine. This is just our clever mind justifying its wrong actions, but with this attitude we will just continue doing the wrong thing and create more problems. We have to be honest with ourselves.

OVER DRAMATISATION

Part of us likes drama and intrigue. We get a subtle pleasure from the soap opera of life, but there is a danger in over dramatising situations where it is not necessary. We can feed negative situations and make small conflicts escalate beyond all proportion. We stake too much on insignificant issues, often putting others on the spot to make decisions one way or the other.

Don't take everything to heart — small issues will soon blow over — if we allow it.

EMOTIONAL THINKING

Emotions are fleeting. Anger comes and goes. Fear comes and goes. Our emotional state is unreliable guide to the truth of an issue. Many times we are relieved we didn't act out of impulsive anger. To really understand a situation, we have to see it without the cloud of emotion. Take time to see beyond a misleading emotion.

These ways of looking at life all share a common theme : it is easy to gain an unbalanced look at life. When we look at problems through a certain filter it is inevitable that we create problems and have poor perception. To deal with this problem we need to avoid jumping to conclusions and be wary of our initial judgements. Before acting we need to test our state of mind:

- o Are we judging with our critical mind or our compassionate heart?
- o How would we want other people to behave or think in our situation?
- o If we spoke out aloud our thoughts, would we be embarrassed about what we are saying?
- o Have we taken a second opinion from other people we trust?
- o Why are we being determined to see the negative side of life?

HOW TO GET THINGS DONE

There is an old saying "If you want something done, ask a busy person." There is a lot of truth in this. Sometimes, we struggle to do anything productive even if we have time on our hands, whilst at other times we can do a lot because we prepare, focus and do it with enthusiasm. There are several small things that can make a big difference to how successful we become. These are some tips to help get things done.

BE CLEAR WHAT YOU WANT TO DO

It might seem a rather obvious point, but if we are not clear what we want to do, how can we do it effectively? I have a student who always talks of giving up smoking. Half of him wants to stop, but the other half enjoys it. If you want to do something difficult like give up smoking you have to be 100 percent committed. If you do something but are holding onto reservations, you will not be fully committed and so it will be much harder, if not impossible. Too often we drift along with vague ideas that we should be doing something; we hold a certain guilt for not doing it, but we fail to clearly resolve to take action — so it gets left on the back burner.

CLEAR OUT THE JUNK

One of the biggest obstacles to being productive is getting distracted by small silly things. Having a tidy workspace makes a big difference to being able to work with great focus. Entering a clear, simple work environment gives a definite subconscious psychological boost. Just try tidying your workspace, ruthless clearing out the junk and pieces of paper — you will definitely notice the difference. We may have a rather romantic view of the eccentric genius working in paper strewn mess coming up with complex equations,but for most of us, working in this kind of environment makes it much more difficult to do anything. Investing ten minutes to create a clear workspace is a good investment of time.

DO ONE THING AT A TIME

It is not possible to do more than one thing at a time and be focused, so our attention becomes split and we struggle to do either task effectively. This doesn't just mean physically doing only one thing at a time; it also means having our thoughts focused on one particular task. When writing an essay, we need to ignore other thoughts of what we will be doing tomorrow. There is no benefit in worrying about things that we have no control over.

BE IN THE RIGHT ENVIRONMENT

As we have mentioned in previous points, the real secret for getting things done is being 100 percent committed and focused. Another thing that can help is being in the right environment. For example, if you need to work at home, create a suitable space for your work. If you carry your laptop into the lounge in front of the TV, you can get easily distracted. Even changing clothes can make a difference. Sometimes, I wander out into the garden in my slippers and start half-heartedly gardening but am very unproductive. When you do something, be in the right space, environment and with the right tools/equipment.

PRIORITISE

The art of getting things done doesn't mean we have to be a permanent hive of activity, business and stress. The problem is that we are often "busy" doing unimportant and inconsequential things. We need to make a list (either written or mental) of what needs doing and then doing the most pressing things first, even if it is not necessarily the most pleasant.

Feel that whatever you do there is an opportunity cost. If we spend time flicking through tv channels, it means we don't have time for something more fulfilling and worthwhile.

FINISH WHAT YOU START

The hardest thing with getting things done is often just getting started. It takes a mental effort to get started, so once you overcome this barrier, try finishing it in one go. If we keep stopping and starting, we will waste precious time and lose focus. Where possible, try to benefit from economies of scale, e.g. rather than checking emails several times throughout the day, set aside one or two times to answer and deal with your inbox. This is more efficient than responding piecemeal to incoming messages (and often when you are trying to do something else as well).

READ THE INSTRUCTION MANUAL

It's a bit of novelty in our ipod generation, but so many times I try to do something without any preparation, find that I make it worse and then have to go back to read the instruction manual. Good preparation can save a lot of heartache and wasted effort. Jumping straight in without any clear plan isn't usually the best way to get something done.

BE ENTHUSIASTIC FOR WHAT YOU DO

If we can always maintain enthusiasm for what we do, our enthusiasm will carry us through all obstacles and problems. This is a real secret of getting things done.

THE ART OF DOING NOTHING

"I used to have a son who sat around doing nothing, but then he took up meditation." It's a rather feeble New Age joke, but the idea of doing nothing sounds rather shocking, yet doing nothing can be one of the most rewarding things. Here, doing nothing doesn't mean loafing away, idly passing time. Doing nothing means the willingness to switch off from external distractions and worries. It means being happy to be in our present surroundings and at peace with ourself.

TIME TO YOURSELF

We may spend a great deal of time looking after our family or commuting to work; we may work 8 hours a day for a boss. Why do we find it so difficult to spend 15–20 minutes to ourselves?

DON'T BE AFRAID OF SILENCE

We have become afraid of our own selves, and afraid of silence. We have become accustomed to absorbing ourselves in external distractions, often looking at a screen. Because we never spend time with ourselves, we become frightened of what we might find. Real silence is relaxing and reinvigorating. We need to learn to be at peace with ourselves. We must avoid the temptation to start judging ourselves and other people and just be in peace.

LESS IS MORE

We often have a feeling that we need to try and control everything. We need to change others behaviour, we need to change ourselves, we need to change the world. We expend a lot of energy ruminating over the failings of others and what they ought to do. Often this is just on a mental level. Our thoughts are filled with what other people should do and why they are bad. In fact, in many cases we would be better off just minding our own business. There are many things that we are not responsible for, especially when it comes to changing other people. We can inspire them and lead by example, but sometimes we need to allow people to make their own choices and follow their own path. In that area we should be happy to do nothing. We can offer people our good will, but we should not feel responsible for their mistakes.

DOING NOTHING WITH A PURPOSE

We are doing nothing when we surf through the internet, watch some daytime cooking programme or check our emails for a record 16th time in the past two hours. We can be in the vortex of activity but achieve nothing meaningful. The problem is we rush into activity without any preparation or thought. The art of doing nothing involves gaining an inner preparation, a mental stillness and cultivating an inner peace which gives meaning to our outer life. Meditation is the active cultivation of this inner silence and inner peace. It is the best way to gain a meaningful inner peace.

We can also just be more aware of the simplicity of life and nature. If we pursue simplicity and awareness we will appreciate many simple things much more.

PART VII

THE MIND-JUNGLES AND
THE HEART-GARDENS OF LIFE

Sri Chinmoy

A DROP OF KINDNESS BECOMES THE SEA

T HERE WAS ONCE a very, very old man who was extremely poor. He could not find work as, at that time, there was a serious problem with unemployment. Even young people could not find jobs. Who would give a job to an old man?

He said to himself, "I am unemployed and have only one dollar left." Then he heard that somebody had a job for an old man to be a gatekeeper. The person said that only an old man would be hired for this job and that the person would have to do next to nothing. It was the perfect job for an old man. The old man was so hopeful.

At that moment, a beggar came by and asked the old man for some money. The old man thought, "Tomorrow I have to look for a job. But now this beggar is here. What am I going to do?"

The old man could see from the beggar's face and eyes that he was famished. The old man thought, "All right. What can I do?" He gave half his dollar to the beggar saying, "Let us share equally. I am giving you half of my money, and I am keeping the other half.

The gatekeeper job that the old man was applying for was quite far from his house, so he took the bus. He thought he could ride the bus all the way there. Alas, the old man had gone only half-way, when the bus driver said, "Your ride is over here. Now you have to get off, because you only paid fifty cents." He had no more money, because he had given the beggar fifty cents the day before.

The old man started walking and walking. The place was still quite far away. His mind was saying, "Why did I give away my money to the beggar?" But his heart was very happy saying, "With my little money, just fifty cents, perhaps the beggar was able to get a sandwich." The mind said he did the wrong thing and heart said he did the right thing. A very nice argument was going on between the old man's mind and heart.

Just then, a middle-aged man approached the old man and said, "You are so old and so tired. What are you doing? You seem so exhausted; why are you walking? Please come and rest inside my house."

The old man said, "No. No. I have to go. I am looking for a job. Somebody told me that there is a gatekeeper job and they are looking for an old person to do it. That is why I am going there. I have such a long way still to go."

The other man said, "No! You do not have to go anywhere else. Come to my house. I will give you a job. But first, please eat. Every day you will come to my house and you will do a very simple job. By the way, where do you live?"

"I live quite far away from here."

"Do you have any relatives?"

"No, I do not have any relatives."

"Then my house is yours. You stay here. You are free to do whatever you want to do. You become the boss and keep the house clean in your own way. I have a big family, and I am taking you as our grandfather."

The old man said to his new boss, "Yesterday I gave fifty cents to a very poor man. I showed just a little kindness to a poor beggar. Today you have given me the whole world. You are inundating me with a sea of kindness, affection and love."

Sri Chinmoy

THE OLD MAN'S CURE FOR THE MAIDSERVANT'S VANITY

A YOUNG MAIDSERVANT came regularly to clean the house of an old man. One day, the young lady was crying and crying. The old man said, "Why are you crying? I will gladly give you money, if that is what you need."

"I do not need money. I am upset because I am so vain. Since I feel I am very beautiful, every day I look at myself in the mirror. I appreciate my beauty and adore myself. This is not good at all!"

The old man said, "Please do not worry!"

"But I know that it is a sin to appreciate one's beauty excessively. I spend so much time looking in the mirror. I look at my eyes, my hair and everything. How beautiful I am! But it is such a sin to be as vain as I am."

The old man replied, "No, no! It is not a sin. It is only a mistake. Just do not make the same mistake again."

The maidservant said, "I cannot get out of this habit. Every day I have to spend so much time appreciating my limbs, hair, nose, ears, eyes — everything. What can I do?"

The old man offered his advice. "You know that I am an old man. I have lost all my hair, and I am not at all beautiful. In a few years, I shall die. I am so old! You love me so much, and I love you so much. What you can do is, when you look in the mirror, immediately think of me. Imagine that my face is on the other side. Imagine my face with wrinkles everywhere. See my bald head and think of my eyes and my face."

She said, "I have such love and admiration for you. You are my boss. You know how much I love and adore you. How can I do that?"

"No, you can do it. If you think of me with all your love, you will be able to see me in the mirror and not yourself."

The maidservant said, "I simply cannot do it."

The old man said, "All right. Do not listen to me. Go and appreciate your beauty for hours. What I do not understand is how you can come on time every day."

"Every morning I get up very early so I will have plenty of time to look in the mirror and see just how beautiful I am; then I come to your house. Every day I have been committing so many sins!"

Her boss said, "I already told you that this is just a mistake. Do not worry about it. If you really want to solve your problem, then do exactly what I have suggested."

She said, "All right. Tomorrow I shall try."

The following morning, the maidservant looked in the mirror and thought of her boss. Then she saw an old face, with wrinkled skin and no hair. She said to herself, "This is terrible! I do not want to see this!"

When she got to work, the maidservant said, "Boss! Boss! You have saved me! Today I did not spend any time in front of the mirror. On other days I usually spend at least half an hour appreciating my beauty. Today, as soon as I looked in the mirror, I was able to see you. Then I lost all my inspiration to look in the mirror. While we are here together, I see how kind, compassionate and loving you are. But while I was looking in the mirror, I did not like what I saw at all!"

The boss said, "I am so happy. I have given you the medicine. Every day, when you look in the mirror, I will solve your problem. You will see me there — just how ugly I am — and you will not have to waste your precious time. You will definitely be able to fully overcome your vanity."

Sri Chinmoy

THE BUSINESSMAN FINDS
HAPPINESS IN SMILES

A BUSINESSMAN was very, very rich. Unlike other rich men, he was very kindhearted. Always he was giving away money, offering charity, helping his friends and serving others through many self-giving deeds. Compared to other businessmen, this man was a real exception. He kept next to nothing of his own money for his own needs. Whatever extra he earned through his business, he gave away.

The man's business was really prospering. One day, a friend of the businessman asked him, "Can you not keep a little more money for yourself?"

The businessman replied, "That I cannot do. Whatever little I need, I take. The other money that I have earned, I am giving away, because I do not need any extra. I want people to be happy. There are so many people who are very, very poor. When I have money and I spend it, I do get joy. But when others are using my money and getting joy, I get so much more joy.

"When I walk along the street in the morning, if I see all sad faces, then I feel miserable. Instead, now I am seeing that these people are becoming happy with my money. I am seeing so many smiling faces. Along Eternity's Road, if I can make people happy, then I am the happiest person. My happiness does not depend on money. It is only in giving and in becoming one with others' joy. Happiness for me is to see another person's smiling face and satisfied heart."

This businessman learned that he could be very, very happy by making others happy. He was a businessman, but he was also a deeply spiritual man. He was doing his business and depending fully on God's Grace.

REFERENCES

1. Sri Chinmoy, *Peace*, New York: Agni Press, 1985.
2. Paramahansa Yogananda, *Inner Peace — How to be Calmly Active and Actively Calm*, Los Angeles: Self-Realization Fellowship, 1999.
3. Thomas Jefferson, *Letter to the Infant Thomas Jefferson Smith*, 21 February 1825.
4. Sri Chinmoy, *The Illumination Of Life-Clouds*, Part 2, New York: Agni Press, 1974.
5. Sri Chinmoy, *Ten Thousand Flower-Flames*, Part 77, #7666. New York: Agni Press, 1983 .
6. Sri Chinmoy, *Seventy-Seven Thousand Service-Trees*, Part 13, #12753. New York: Agni Press, 1999.
7. Sri Chinmoy, *Twenty-Seven Thousand Aspiration-Plants*, #14805. Part 149, New York: Agni Press, 1991.
8. William Shakespeare, *All's Well That Ends Well*, Act I, Scene I, 1601
9. Sri Chinmoy, *Earth's Cry Meets Heaven's Smile*, Part 1, New York: Agni Press, 1974.
10. Leonardo Da Vinci, *The Notebooks of Leonardo da Vinci*, English translation by Jean Paul Richter, 1888
11. Sri Chinmoy, *Inner Progress And Satisfaction-Life*, New York: Agni Press, 1977.

12. Sri Chinmoy, *Ten Thousand Flower-Flames*, Part 12, #1120. New York: Agni Press, 1981.

13. Sri Chinmoy, *Sri Chinmoy Seventy-Seven Thousand Service-Trees*, Part 19, #18362. New York: Agni Press, 2000.

14. William Shakespeare, *Sonnets*, Sonnet 116, 1609

15. Sri Chinmoy, *Earth's Cry Meets Heaven's Smile*, Part 3, New York: Agni Press, 1978.

16. Sri Chinmoy, *A Soulful Cry Versus A Fruitful Smile*, New York: Agni Press, 1977.

17. Sri Chinmoy, *Seventy-Seven Thousand Service-Trees*, Part 15, #14779. New York: Agni Press, 1999.

18. Sri Chinmoy, *Fifty Freedom-Boats To One Golden Shore*, Part 2, New York: Agni Press, 1974.

19. Sri Chinmoy, *Earth's Cry Meets Heaven's Smile*, Part 1, New York: Agni Press, 1974.

20. Sri Chinmoy, *My Flute*, #1. New York: Agni Press, 1972.

21. Sri Chinmoy, *Life-Tree-Leaves*, New York: Agni Press, 1974.

22. George Bernard Shaw, *Man and Superman*, act 4, 1903

23. Sri Chinmoy, *The Mind-Jungles and The Heart-Gardens of Life*, Parts I and Parts VII, New York: Agni Press, 2001

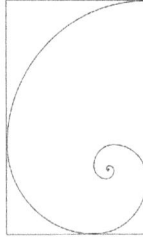

Many thanks to
Prof. Enrico Gregorio,
For his invaluable advice on
The advanced use of TEX e XƎLATEX.

TYPESETTING WAS HAND-CODED WITH TEX AND XƎLATEX BY γ.ς. [LYON, LXXXI S.C.E.]

www.ingramcontent.com/pod-product-compliance
Lightning Source LLC
Chambersburg PA
CBHW020517100426
42813CB00030B/3285/J